# DANCEFLOOR DREAMS

## A Bride's Guide to the Perfect Wedding

### DAVID CAMPO

Hardcover ISBN 979-8-9932857-0-2
Paperback ISBN 979-8-9932857-1-9
Ebook ISBN 979-8-9932857-2-6

Cover design: Becca Smith
Interior design: Jon Hahn Design

Printed in the United States of America

First and foremost and most importantly, this book is dedicated to God. He has me where I believe I'm supposed to be. I credit everything to Him because He put the passion and the drive within me a long time ago and brought me to an entirely different level. Thank you, Father.

This book is also dedicated to my wife Karee, who always supported me through this musical journey of mine and who has been by my side from the first word in this book to the last; to my daughter Kaycee, who inspires me every time I see an emotional father/daughter dance where I envision the day where I'll get to be "that dad" instead of the DJ; to my son Charles, who has helped me so much over the years, from hauling equipment to teaching me better ways to rock the mic to helping me find my inner voice; and to my son Quinn, who is on his own musical journey of a different kind—I'd like to think you got your love of music from me, so learn everything you can and reach for the stars.

This book also wouldn't have happened without all of the brides over the years who trusted me with their weddings. Because of you, I gained an incredible amount of knowledge and experience over the course of each event. So to all of my couples and your families: a sincere thank-you.

# CONTENTS

———— ∞∞∞ ————

# ACKNOWLEDGMENTS

*M*ANY THANKS TO THE WONDERFUL VENDORS who took time out of their busy schedules to contribute their insights to this book (and who put up with my persistence as well): Todd Schott of Chopin Mon Ami Caterers in Galveston, Texas; Joe Lewis of Joe Lewis Photography in Buffalo, New York; Courtney Parker of Queenie Designs in Houston, Texas; Christina Muehle, the Venue Manager of The Lyceum in Galveston, Texas; and Jula Tragni of Cakes By Jula in Galveston, Texas.

And of course I would also like to thank the wonderful couples who lent me their innermost thoughts: Jennifer, Amy, Lauren and Caleb, Jordan, Macy, Ali, Rachel, Nick and Kylie, and Clint and Angela.

# INTRODUCTION

Photo by Pro-Stock Studio/Shutterstock, ID: 1064906999

$\mathcal{S}$o, YOU'RE ENGAGED AND ON THE verge of planning a wedding, or maybe you've even started the process already. The engagement is filled with so much excitement you can hardly stand it, and you just cannot wait to get going. But between the time of your engagement and the time you actually start booking vendors, your excitement can quickly die down once you start receiving quotes and looking at the overall cost of just how much your dream wedding will be. The wedding business is huge. Though there will always be a need for it—just like there will always be a need for insurance, funerals, real estate, and transportation—once those dollar signs start popping up, you may start looking at other options and figuring out where you can cut costs.

So many brides go into these first stages of wedding planning completely blind. Sure, there are great resources and information readily available, but you can get overwhelmed fast. There are hundreds of different wedding websites with their own way of doing things. But hopefully, this book will help you make wise decisions about booking your DJ and other vendors. I'll be honest with you about what to look out for and what to avoid; I'll provide sample questions to ask your DJ (and how to know if you're just getting an earful of excuses) and will also clue you in on how to make confident decisions. If nothing else, I sincerely hope this book gives you a little more insight into real-life wedding planning and helps you enter this process with a better picture of exactly what you want and how you want it done. My main goal is to help you avoid mistakes—whether that's simply a bad vendor or something as catastrophic as a tumultuous wedding night.

Years ago, growing up, my plan was to be a fiction writer. My aunt once told me to "write what you know," and the only thing I've really known for the more than two decades is being a wedding DJ. I've been in the business for over 20 years, and I've learned a lot, seen a lot, and heard a lot. There have been things I've done right, things I've had to correct, and things I thought about doing but never did. With each wedding, I get better and better. I've changed the way I handle timelines, and I've learned to always have backups of everything, from equipment to mics to music. I've learned to *always* listen to songs purchased from iTunes, just to make sure (because even though it says "clean radio edit," that doesn't necessarily mean dirty words aren't lurking in there somewhere). I've learned ways to help brides streamline the process of online planning and building their request lists. With all the information that I've acquired, it would be a waste not to share it with every bride that I can reach. This is my first reason for writing this book.

The second reason is due to the horror stories I've heard about brides having a terrible wedding experience. Maybe it's because the DJ they hired wasn't worth the time, money, or aggravation, or maybe it's because the coordinator didn't know what they were doing. Maybe the photographer left before the formal dances took place. Believe me, I've seen it all. And now it's my mission to reveal to you, the bride, exactly what a wonderful wedding can be like from a DJ's perspective, since I've worked more weddings than you've probably been to! (But more on that later.) I have nothing to lose, and you have everything to gain. So I'm ready to spill my very best secrets to help you make the most of your special day.

Most DJs don't want to reveal their own secrets, but it's so important to me that your special day is exactly what it's meant to be: special. That being said, the words contained here are strictly *my* opinions, and no other DJ companies were harmed during the writing of this book.

# 1

---

# From Passion
# to Profession

Photo by Edward Olive/Dreamstime, ID 55188377

To BE A GOOD DJ, A PERSON has to know a wide range of music. Not just the current hits—they have to *really* know music. A DJ just starting out, especially if they're young, might know all of the club mixes, all of the latest hip-hop tracks and most danceable tunes, and that's great, but to do the wedding circuit, a DJ has to know everything from the 1940s to the 2000s, and everything from country to disco to Spanish music. A DJ has to be able to zero in on a song that can be paired perfectly with whatever is currently playing, and he or she has to know when to back off the energy and throw in a slow song or two.

I can't really narrow down when I started really loving music, but I know I started at an early age. My grandmother used to play the old *Romper Room* 45 records that accompanied a follow-along book, and that's probably where it started, somewhere in the early 1970s. By 1976 I was hooked on the radio and trying to tape record songs as they played live on the air, all the while hoping that the DJ wouldn't talk over the intro of whatever song I was trying to record. By 1983, I accidentally found *Casey Kasem's American Top 40* radio countdown and followed it faithfully until about mid-1986.

After taking a radio/television broadcast class at Ball High School during my senior year in 1984, I landed a weekend job at the old radio station KGBC in Galveston, Texas. My job was to work on Sundays playing commercials from an 8-track machine during the NASCAR races, and then when those races ended, I was supposed to play country music for the listeners. The disc jockey that came in after me for his show would bring in his Pat Benatar and Journey albums to play, and this was the music that I was grooving to, not the Merle Haggard and Buck Owens tunes that I was spinning. I thought, *if he can do it, why can't I?* Well, I didn't take into consideration the listening audience, who, during my shift were in the 60- and 70-something age group. The next week I played Quiet Riot and Prince, and apparently the station owner was listening at the time. By the following week, I was out of a job. At least it ended with a bang.

Fast forward to the year 2001. At a friend's class reunion, the DJ put on "Play That Funky Music," and I thought, *Hey, I could do that!* After all, I had tons of CDs after building my collection throughout the '90s thanks to Columbia House's 10-disks-for-a-penny deal (using different names under different accounts, most of which ended up in credit collection). But I was loaded with music, and all those CDs were just sitting at home collecting dust. So, I walked up to the DJ and offered my services, should he ever need an assistant. A few months later, I got a call from that DJ and the next thing I knew, I was now an assistant DJ. I'd watch and learn, seeing what he was playing and when, how he interacted with the crowd, what he said on the mic, and how much energy he used. I learned everything I could and eventually broke away to launch my own business.

It was hard in the beginning, scratching out every birthday party I could beg for, doing charity events, and trying to figure it all out. I started doing a lot of class reunions, and although it paid the bills, it didn't move me. Some of them were fun because I got to research the music of any given class's graduation year, but it was just a gig. What I *really* wanted to do was the wedding circuit. Once I booked and worked my first wedding reception, I was hooked.

In the beginning, I would get such a bad case of butterflies because, when I stopped to really think about it, I realized the entire success (or failure) of the event sat heavily on my shoulders. I either had to have the skill to make the party sizzle or the stupidity of not knowing enough to ruin it. There were many times early on when my wife learned not to bother me before a gig—I was *that* tuned into the bride's day.

Two decades later, now it runs like clockwork. I've gained enough experience to know how to make a party fun, but it didn't come easy. Call me modest, but I've always credited the success of the wedding to the people that are in it, whether it's the parents, the wedding party, or the guests. A DJ can play the biggest hits, the best line dances, and the hottest remixes, but if people aren't feeling it, they aren't feeling it, and there's nothing he or she can do about it.

Some DJs tend to get annoyed when they're playing something and a wedding guest asks for a specific song. Who knows, maybe their ego took a hit because they played *someone else's* request and that got everybody back out on the floor. But I always encourage requests. Maybe someone knows a song that the bride loved in college, and they remember her playing it over and over on her phone. Here's the one thing that I learned early on: The people at the wedding know more about the bride than the DJ does. And that's why a DJ has to be open to what guests want to hear. A DJ has to be on board with what *the crowd* want to hear, not what *he* wants to hear. You, as the bride knows what you want, and if the DJ goes in the opposite direction, then he's not truly seeing your vision.

# 2

---

# Why Hire a DJ?

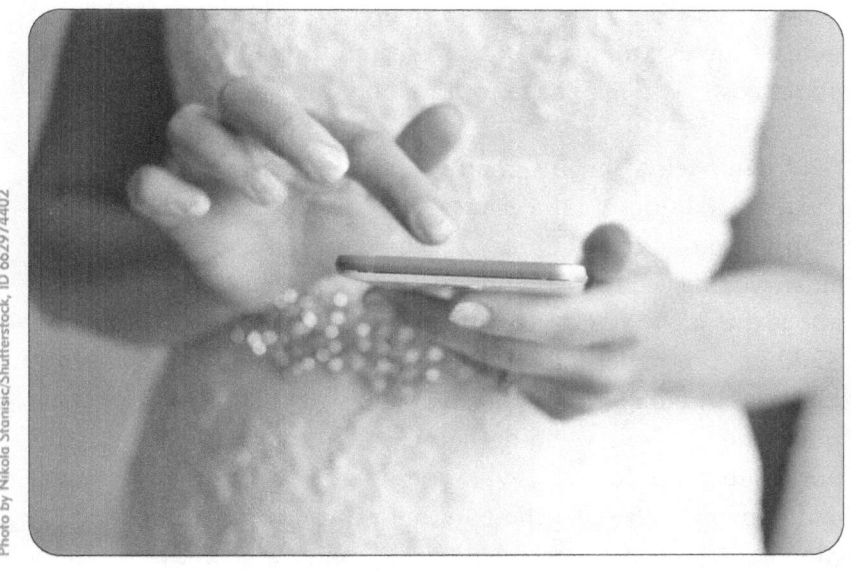

*B*ACK IN THE DAY, THERE WAS NO such thing as an *iPod wedding*. Now, I'm sure that plenty of couples have successfully used their phones, iPads, tablets, and other devices to replace the common DJ. If it's an informal and basic get-together being celebrated in someone's backyard, maybe that would work, but it definitely won't fly in a ballroom or at a proper event venue. Friends and family members doing you a favor simply aren't trained in the wedding business. Sure, anyone can pull up Apple Music and put a bunch of songs in a playlist; anyone can bring a Bluetooth speaker and connect a mic to it. But it's just not worth sacrificing good quality sound only to save a few bucks. *All* guests at the event should be enjoying the evening, not spending it running back and forth to the speaker, grabbing their phone, and pressing play on a song that they *think* will be a danceable hit. Not to mention—what if this friend didn't put his or her phone in airplane mode? Guess what, all of their notifications will be coming in, interrupting the music. And if they're using the free version of Spotify, you'll get the commercials in between songs too.

I get it: Weddings are expensive. The best day of your life is going to cost you. You have to figure out a budget, and if that budget forces you to make certain adjustments and decisions about costs, you may have to skimp on one thing or another. So, what suffers?

I can't tell you how many stories I've heard about brides cheaping out on a DJ because the couple didn't think it was worth spending more money on the music. But the way I see it, either you decide to hire a great DJ and your guests will be raving about the music at your wedding for years to come, or you spend $200 on a beginner and your guests will still be talking about it for years to come—only not in a good way. Having your sister's boyfriend DJ your wedding because he "knows good music" is not a substitute for a DJ who does this for a living every weekend. Anyone can push the play button, but only a qualified DJ can read the room, see what's happening, and know when to transition to a different song or a different genre. Beyond just the music, a good DJ will also have quality sound and lighting systems, won't take breaks, and will be sure to stay at their setup all night long with a live mic available whenever announcements, whether sudden or planned, need to be made.

I cannot express enough the importance of hiring a professional DJ, and hiring a good one. You're handing *them* the job of handling your wedding day soundtrack so *you* don't have to worry about it.

I asked Macy, a bride who was referred to me by a family friend to DJ her wedding, what her thoughts were on her wedding day:

Brides should know that my wedding day did not go any way I honestly expected it to; it was better! When I first started planning my wedding, I had planned it going one way and had every single thing planned down to a T for who was going to be in what position, and then everything went awry. But, my next-door neighbor got me in touch with this awesome DJ who not only could DJ my wedding but also officiated it! He had no problem going with our crazy theme of *Star Wars* and tailored our vows special just for us, but as a twist, we had no idea what we were going to say until we were standing face-to-face, getting ready to say "I do." If you can take away anything from my wedding day, it's to just go with it, because you may have one thing planned and something may go wrong, but it may be just what you needed to happen to have the best wedding day of your life!

And this is why it's so important to let a professional handle the music for your wedding instead of someone not trained in the industry.

# 3

---

# A DJ or a Band?

ANOTHER DECISION YOU MAY NEED TO MAKE regarding the music for your wedding is whether you want to hire a DJ or a band . . . or both.

I've worked weddings with bands where they were the main entertainment, and I was just the background sound during the band's breaks. But there's always been that awkward tension between DJs and musicians, mostly coming from the musician's point of view: *You're playing other people's music while we're actually playing our own instruments and singing.* Not all band members think this way, but there's still that potential for awkwardness. Yet from the DJ's point of view, some of them may be thinking, *You guys get to take breaks, not to mention I play the original songs that people easily recognize.* Though again, not all DJs that think this way.

I wouldn't say it's a war between the two, but there are definitely differences between bands and DJs. Though I certainly won't try to persuade you one way or the other, in this chapter I'm going to give you all the information you need to make a decision about what arrangement will work best for you.

Let's start with the band. When they're playing, people will dance as long as what they're playing sounds good. A good band can play a variety. But can they take requests? Only if it's in their set list. They can have a large library of songs that they play, but if a guest wants to hear something that they don't know, then that guest is out of luck. The music will also be *LOUD*. It has to be in order for all the instruments and the vocals to be in sync. Guests, especially older ones, may not want to be around the amped-up music unless they're out on the floor dancing. Though I've also never seen a guest go up to a band member and ask them to turn down the volume like they do with a DJ because they know all the DJ has to do is move a slider on his or her mixer.

For example, I worked a wedding not too long ago where the couple had me as their DJ and they also had a band there. The venue itself was a rectangular-shaped ballroom, where the stage was on the right side, with tables on either side. They put me way in the far end of the room since I wasn't the main source of the music; my job was just to play during the band's breaks and then again later when the dancing kicked in. Fortunately, the band arrived early and did their sound checks before the wedding got under way, but I was so far away from everything that I really had to push my speakers to get enough sound across the tables and all the way over to where the dance floor was set up. Of course, whenever possible, a DJ always likes to be somewhere close to the dance floor, otherwise the tables directly in front of their area will get blasted out.

In contrast to a band, a DJ *can* play requests (well, depending on how extensive their own music library is). A DJ can also play originals that most people relate to. For instance, the well-known version of "Brick House" by the Commodores tends to get the crowd going in a way that five old guys with long beards trying to play it might not; a cover version just doesn't sound or feel the same. True, a DJ isn't quite as exciting to watch as a singer or guitar player. But on the flip side of that, DJs usually don't take breaks; they tend to play from start to finish.

I certainly don't hate working with bands, and when we're booked for the same event I will of course step aside to let them have whatever electrical power they need, as well as the best place to set up. They have lots of cords and cables; I have, at the most, two. They have to sound check every instrument and mic, whereas the only sound check I need to perform is on my mic and speakers.

For example, I was working a wedding once where I was contracted to play at the couple's reception for four hours, ending at 9 p.m. But I also knew there was a band coming in to start their set *beginning* at 9. There was a stage at this venue, and although I could have set up on the stage, I elected to set up across the dance floor and give the band full access to the stage and all the power. Besides, if I *had* set up on the stage, I would've probably had to move anyway. My thoughts are that when a DJ and a band are sharing the spotlight, they should both do their best to work with each other and not argue over who gets what. Anyway, around 7-ish, the band arrives and starts setting up; a little bit later, they start sound checking their mics. The drummer starts banging away on his drums and the noise is drowning out the music that I was playing. As a drummer myself, I know it takes time to get everything set up, tuned, and sounding good, but the problem was doing it while I as the DJ was doing *my job*. I just think that both the DJ and the band should have done their sound checks *before* the wedding.

So there it is. Bands versus DJs. I will say that it *is* possible for bands and DJs to work together for a common good: the success of the wedding and the happiness of the bride. Some couples hire both, some don't. Now it's up to you to decide which is best for *your* wedding.

# 4

---

# Interviewing the DJ

*N*OW THAT YOU'VE DECIDED ON HIRING A DJ instead of asking Uncle Jasper to run music from his iPhone 5, the first thing to consider is what questions to ask your professional DJ candidates. In this chapter, we'll take a look at the most popular questions couples have asked me, and hopefully it'll generate other questions you may choose to ask.

*Tip: Make a long list of everything you want to ask.*

A welcoming DJ who *truly* wants your business will answer *any and all* questions you have, from the contract details to the deposit to the after-event follow-up. Don't feel like you have to pick and choose certain questions to ask because you don't want to annoy them. You are doing this once, and they only get one chance to impress *you*.

♪ ♪ ♪ ♪

But before you interview *any* DJ, you need to decide on how many total hours you'll need them for. From my experience in the Houston-based wedding circuit, between four and five hours is perfect, even with a ceremony. Anything over six hours, you're probably just wasting your money, especially if it's a weekday wedding or a Sunday event. Can weddings go beyond six hours? It's happened before, and it's not unheard of, but remember, less is more. Of course, the number of hours you choose will also depend on which events you have planned, the size of your venue, how many guests are coming, etc. If you're having 200 people in a large ballroom and you have everything from formal dances to dinner games to the tosses, then maybe six hours of music will work for you. But by the same token, if you have only 60 people invited, then there's really no need to go beyond four or five hours.

Here's the thing: Schedule your DJ for between four and five hours, and then if the party is still going strong, pay your DJ overtime. It's impossible to foresee whether your guests will leave early or stay until the end until you're actually there. Besides, you don't know what music your DJ will be playing; that music will either entice guests to stay and dance or to leave early because the music (or the DJ) sucks.

Regardless, my policy (and most other DJs will agree with me on this) is that I don't give refunds on unused time. If a couple hires me to DJ their ceremony and reception from 5 p.m. until midnight, yet by 11 p.m. there are only six guests left, none of whom are dancing, that does not constitute grounds for a refund. That's just throwing your money away. Like I said, less is more.

When trying to figure out times, set aside a time that you would like to have for open dancing. Then build your timeline around that portion and figure out when you want the formal dances, dinner/cake/toasts, and the bouquet and/or garter tosses to happen, if you're also having those. From there you should be able to pinpoint how many hours you'll need.

Here are a couple of scenarios to give you an idea of how to decide on start-to-finish times.

## Wedding #1, 4 Hours

- Ceremony starts at 4 p.m.
- Cocktail hour starts at 4:30 p.m.
- Couple/wedding party introduced at 5:30 p.m.
- First dance right after the grand entrance.
- Dinner starts at 5:45 p.m.
- Cake cutting and toasts follow at 6:15 or 6:30 p.m.
- Parent dances at around 6:45 or 7 p.m.
- Open dancing from 7 to 8:30 p.m.
- Tosses anywhere between 8 and 8:30 p.m.
- Last dance at around 8:45 p.m.
- The couple's send-off at 9 p.m.

As you can tell from the above mock timeline, the couple has about an hour and a half of dance time, which is actually a good amount of time. Cocktail hours usually last anywhere from 30 minutes to an hour, depending on how many pictures your photographer is taking of the wedding party.

We can also assume that dinner service will usually be around 30 minutes for a buffet line, sometimes longer for a plated dinner. Cutting the cake doesn't usually take too long, and depending on how many people you have lined up for the toasts, this portion of the night can take up 15 to 20 minutes. The parent dances (if you're having them) don't take up too much time, and then you're ready for the dance portion. And if you're having the tosses, they can be inserted anywhere toward the end. Scheduling the last dance 15 minutes before the end gives your guests enough time to collect their belongings and head for the door, then your send-off is right at 9.

## Wedding #2: 6 Hours

- Ceremony starts at 5 p.m.
- Cocktail hour starts at 5:30 p.m.
- Couple/wedding party introduced at 6:30-ish.
- First dance right after the grand entrance.
- Dinner starts at 6:45 p.m.
- Cake cutting and toasts at 7:30 p.m. (at the latest).
- Parent dances begin at 7:45-ish.
- Open dancing starts at 8 p.m.
- Last dance at 10:45 p.m.
- Send-off at 11 p.m.

Let's assume that this couple is not doing any tosses. Just by glancing at this timeline, you can see that you'd have almost three hours of dance time. This timeline doesn't account for any dollar dances you may want to have, for photographer's time in the sunset with the couple, for any unforeseen delays, etc. You just have to research and see what's best for *your* timeline.

———————

Now that you have a clearer idea of how many hours you want for your wedding, step two is to start reaching out to DJ companies. There are so many out there, so you'll have to really do your homework, but be cautious in your search. Anyone can buy speakers, a mic, and a mixer and call themselves a DJ without ever having done a wedding before. So, what makes a DJ unique? And more importantly, how do couples know what DJ is the best fit for them? And what is it that you're paying for?

You're essentially trying to find out why they charge so much or so little. Just because one DJ charges a hundred times more doesn't mean they're worth it. There's no guarantee that spending $2,500 on a DJ instead of hiring one who's charging $200 will be the best fit for your wedding. Do your homework. Read reviews, and do an extensive search online. If you go to a bridal show, collect information, but don't feel like you're being pushed into a contract on the spot.

As the client, you have the right to dictate everything from start to finish. If you don't want any rap played at your reception, then you should be confident in knowing that there won't be any rap played at your reception. All DJs should go by your playlist because it's what *you* want played and what you think your guests will love to dance to. However, there may be songs that a good DJ knows will also be a hit on the dance floor, so you'll want to give them *some* freedom.

When interviewing, be specific. Get to know your DJ—what music they tend to gravitate to, what tracks they know are good dance songs versus what tracks aren't. Quiz them on music: "What country songs do you play the most of and what are your go-to country classics?"

Here are the top questions that I've been asked and that need to be asked in order for you to make a reasonable decision about who gets to play music at your wedding. Feel free to use any of them. I'll also give you some insight on why it's vital to ask these questions.

You're probably thinking, *shouldn't I ask how much they charge first?* Most couples do, but that question won't necessarily be answered right away. You want to find out about their performance and planning process, and *then* you can ask for a price if you like what you've heard thus far. Remember this: A good DJ doesn't compete on price; they compete on experience.

## ❒ *Are you available?*

This question sits at #1 because if they're not available, there's no point in going any further. Don't just ask if someone at their company is available; if you want a specific DJ, ask them if *they* are available, not a side DJ.

And let me just stress something else here. The typical time frame for booking a DJ is anywhere between eight months and a year, sometimes more, sometimes less. Don't ask for quotes from a DJ if you're two years out from your date, because prices change and companies change and so do circumstances. On the same token, don't wait until two weeks before your wedding to book a DJ because by then, even a month before, you'll be desperate and forced to start DJ–dumpster diving.

### ❏ Why should I choose you for my wedding day?

You may get a lot of the same answers for this question. Every DJ you interview will probably say the same thing, only put differently. Some DJs will tell you that they have an awesome music collection, the coolest lights and effects, and they've done a lot of weddings. Another DJ may tell you that they're available and that they have towering speakers and know how to bring the party to the dance floor. Yet another DJ will tell you that they'll go above and beyond to make sure your wedding is all you envisioned, this being possibly the most enticing answer. That's like bait to a fish. Anyone can say that and say that all day long. What you want to know is how they can prove it. *How will they go above and beyond for your wedding, and in what way(s) will they ensure that your wedding is all that you envisioned?*

Here's the thing: DMX and LED lighting are fabulous, but they plug in and do their own thing. Just because a DJ has the best lighting doesn't mean he's the best DJ *for you*. Lights are only on during the course of the open dancing sequence. A DJ's real job is so much more than that. It's how they handle a timeline. It's how they transition from one song to the next. And it's how they read the room and how they follow your wishes for the music.

### ❏ How long have you been DJing weddings?

Don't just ask them, "How long have you been a DJ?" They could say five years, though in those five years they could have just been playing for a bunch of teen parties or backyard barbecues. You need to know how many weddings they've DJ'ed on their own and not as a DJ assistant. Unlike a backyard party where making mistakes isn't that big of a deal, a wedding is different. Tiny mistakes can be overlooked, but major ones, such as not having the song you want for your dance with your dad, are not acceptable. So, always ask how many weddings they've DJ'ed. If you needed surgery, you would want a surgeon that's done a lot of surgeries, not a med-school student.

## ❏ *Do you double book?*

Why is this question important? Because you don't want to hire a DJ who's going to be rushing through your wedding just so they can get to another one they have booked across town. And you really don't want a fill-in DJ to show up at your wedding because the DJ that you originally hired has to leave to get to another event. They should be completely dedicated to your wedding that day, and you should get all of their attention. They also need to be available all day in case you have changes to convey to them, such as information about the venue's operating hours, or really, anything else that would require them to respond in a timely manner. When I make final preparations for a wedding, the day of *and* the day before are dedicated to only them.

## ❏ *Do you emcee the entire event?*

This might sound like a silly question because all DJs are supposed to emcee, but you'd be surprised how many times I get asked this very same question. I always announce everything. A DJ should *always* announce:

- All formal dances;
- Who's giving the blessing of the meal and the table release if it's a buffet;
- The cake cutting;

- The toasts and who's toasting;
- Bouquet and garter tosses;
- The last dance and the last call at the bar;
- What's planned for the send-off and what guests need to know before departure.

These are the main announcements I make, but I also keep my eyes open for certain other things, such as if the guest book hasn't been signed by the majority of guests or if the advice cards haven't been filled out. A good DJ should always scan the room to keep guests informed about things like that.

If a DJ wants to charge you extra for extra announcements, you need to say, "Thank you, next."

## ❏ Are you *the one* who will be DJing my wedding?

Their answer to this question could be a make-or-break for you. They'll either say "Yes, I'm the one that will be handling your wedding from start to finish" or "I will put your wedding in the capable hands of one of our awesome DJs" (which means no). And just because they say yes doesn't mean it won't end up in the hands of one of their other DJs anyway if something bigger comes along that they need to be at.

When I started working for that DJ in 2001, I didn't stay around long enough to be sent out to weddings—except one. And I was completely lost. I didn't feel that personalized connection with the couple because all of the details and the music were just handed to me that day. I was totally missing that sense of being able to feel out the bride's vibe or connect with her tastes and personality. Most larger DJ companies book a ton of weddings and send out different DJs to do each of them, and maybe some of them put that DJ in contact with the couple beforehand. Every DJ company is different. But when I started my own company, I made sure to connect with every one of my couples so that I knew exactly what they wanted and how they wanted things done. I set up consultations with them so that we could go over every event in the itinerary.

I personally have loved being a solo entrepreneur, mostly because I know for certain that couples are booking me for my talents, music knowledge, and energy. I've often thought of hiring out DJs to do weddings. I can teach setups; I can teach the ins and outs of timelines and details. But what I can't teach is years of music training. I can hear a song, say, anything by Frank Sinatra or Dean Martin and just know, OK, this would sound great for dinner music or at the beginning of cocktail hour to get people in the mood to dance. I can't really teach that, the ability to read the crowd and know what to play when. That comes from experience.

## ☐ Do you have a backup DJ in the event that you can't make it?

Life throws us all curveballs, and life doesn't care if you have a wedding planned or not, and that includes DJs. You definitely need to ask what happens if the DJ you picked out can't make it. This doesn't mean they just have the sniffles or that a bigger-paying wedding came along on the same date as yours; this means they're dealing with a sudden emergency, an auto accident, an illness, or any other extreme circumstance that would prohibit *the actual DJ that you hired* from playing your wedding. Do they have someone standing by who's not just available to DJ your wedding but is actually *aware* of your wedding songs and the timeline that goes along with them? You need to know that, if your DJ can't show up, someone with a nearly equal amount of experience will be there in their place. If not, you need to know what happens next, before you book.

## ☐ Do you have backup equipment on-site?

Let's say your wedding reception is five hours long. Halfway through, one of your DJ's speakers cuts out. So now the music is only barely filtering through the other speaker, and the guests have clearly noticed the sudden reduction of sound. How do you know the other speaker isn't going to die too? So you ask the DJ if they brought some extra speakers, to which they reply, "My other DJ has the backup equipment at another event." You're screwed.

You should always ask beforehand exactly what kind of backup equipment your DJ will be bringing with them to the wedding. This includes backup speakers, mics, and music-playing devices. Things happen. But don't let it ruin your wedding.

### ☐ *Do you offer lighting packages?*

This is a popular question. For some, it may be something you're not interested in. But if you know for sure that you will want special lighting at your wedding, it can be a definite enhancement. But don't just let the DJ bring whatever lights they think would look good; find out what lighting packages they offer.

Make sure to avoid the strobe lights; you never know if a guest could have a seizure because of the flashing lights. I've had a few couples ask to ensure that I don't bring any. Another thing about lighting is to check with your venue to see if the lights in the room where your reception will be can be turned down or off. If they can't, then there's no point in spending money on lighting because these pretty lights won't have much of an effect if there are bright fluorescents burning above.

Uplighting is a nice effect, and if that's your thing, ask about pricing. If renting uplights looks like it will cost you a small fortune, ask how much the charge would be to just light up one wall or corner, the cake table, or maybe even the DJ booth. Before renting any uplights, though, you should also check with your videographer about colors. Purple and lavender lights will put a cast onto skin tones and make everything look odd. Some videographers will instead suggest a nice orange hue, but that may not be a color you're into.

Don't get talked into fancy lasers and 27 different kinds of lighting effects; a nice, simple lighting setup should be more than enough for your dance floor.

When you ask about lighting, get pricing first without making a verbal agreement to book so that you can compare with other companies. Only then should you make a decision if you even want lights at all.

### ☐ *Do you offer any other add-ons?*

Photo booths, dancing-on-a-cloud machine, and cold spark machine are all add-ons that some DJs will offer.

More than likely, the most expensive option will be the photo booth. However, it will be sure to captivate your audience when there's nothing happening on the dance floor.

The dancing-on-a-cloud machine, otherwise known as a low-lying fog machine, is a great choice for creating the effect of actually dancing on a cloud during your first dance. Venues usually don't mind it because it sticks to the ground and doesn't float up onto the ceiling and risk setting off the automatic sprinkler system like regular fog machines do.

Cold sparks are great for either the grand entrance or the big send-off, and I've even seen some couples use both the fog and the cold sparks during a first dance. It really makes for a memorable experience.

### ☐ *Do you charge for setups and breakdowns?*

If someone charges for a setup or breakdown, move on to the next DJ. Setups and breakdowns should never count as part of your package; it should be something they do on *their time* as part of their wedding preparation. If you want a DJ to play music for five hours and it takes them an additional 90 minutes to get ready, then you're paying for seven hours of music instead of five. Your paid time should begin with the first song played and end with the last song played. Some DJs will act like they're giving you a special deal if their setups and breakdowns are free with a package. They should be free anyway.

## ❏ *Do you charge mileage fees?*

For me personally, the farthest I'll drive without charging mileage is two hours from my location to the couple's venue; that comes to a little over 100 miles. My thought process is that the couple could easily find a DJ company closer to their venue, thereby eliminating me as a possible choice for handling their wedding day. However, then I lose out on what could be another great party and another opportunity for a sparkling review. But other DJs might charge per mile, so it's up to you to assess costs in relation to how much they're already charging you for the DJ package. Some may even have mileage fees already installed in their packages, but if they're charging you mileage to drive 30 minutes to an hour away, I would probably look for another DJ closer to where your venue is. But definitely ask every DJ you interview if there's any mileage charges to your venue.

## ❏ *What's your cancellation policy?*

When planning a wedding, sometimes life happens. Either side can cancel for different reasons. Sometimes things are just out of your control, such as if your venue closes up shop. (It's rare, but it does happen.) But you as the client should know what your DJ's policy is if you have to call things off. How much of your money will you get back?

During the 2020 pandemic, I had signed up to have a booth at a big bridal show in Houston. I was excited and had finally paid off the balance that I owed and was getting everything together for the show that October. It had been a few weeks since I'd heard anything from the company, and my e-mails started going unanswered. Another coordinator contacted me not too long after about the exact same issue they were having, and we came to find out that this company had filed for bankruptcy. They took off with everyone's money, and I was out $1,500. So yes, cancellations can happen at any time, whether it's your choice or someone else's. *Know what your DJ's cancellation policy is before you book, just in case and in the event of.*

I had a bride that booked me a few years ago for her wedding to be held in October, a prime Saturday in the midst of fall. A few months before the wedding, I got a text from her stating that she and her fiancé were choosing to cancel with me without much reason beyond "family issues." She asked me what my cancellation policy was, even though it was all detailed in the contract that we had both signed and had copies of. So, be sure to read the contract before signing it, and ask any and all questions you have up front.

Photo by Kinga/Shutterstock, ID 138342692

If a DJ doesn't allow you to read the contract before putting down a deposit, move on. There may be something in their contract that you aren't on board with, and once you put down money, it may require moving mountains to get it back. Find out what happens if your DJ has to cancel; what happens to your wedding? Find out what happens if unforeseen circumstances force *you* to cancel: What is their policy in that circumstance, and what amount of money you would get back?

In 2008, I booked Amy's wedding after her original DJ cancelled on her. "I don't think I was ever given a reason," she said. "But the emotion was panic. You take a lot of time picking out the right DJ that fits within your budget, and it's hard to find another one on short notice that's available and within your budget. A DJ can make or break your wedding, so it's a big deal to get a good one." Her wedding for me was also memorable in that, just a week later, Hurricane Ike terrorized the entire Gulf Coast. In the days and years following her wedding, we remained friends, and I got to see her and her husband Bobby grow into a family, now with children. What a great love story they had!

There are certain reasons that cancelling (or postponing) a wedding cannot be helped, things that are totally out of your control. Your DJ should take this into consideration when it comes to refunding the amount of money you paid into his or her services. Most deposits are nonrefundable, at least for me they always are, because as a solo DJ, I block out the date so no one else can book it. That deposit holds the date. As for any other payments made toward the balance, refunds are given on a case-by-case basis, depending on the reason(s) that the couple has to cancel. If it's something out of the couple's control, I give them a set amount of time to reschedule. So be sure and check with your DJ and their contract. Again, ask questions before signing anything.

### ❑ *How much is the deposit?*

Jumping off from the above question about cancellations, I'd advise you to also be sure you know how much the deposit is to hold the date and if it's nonrefundable. The deposit could be a small amount that you have to put down, it could be a third or a fourth of the total, or it could even be half, depending on your DJ's policies.

Let's suppose you booked a package for $900, and you paid the entire balance at the time you booked their services. Then, someone in your immediate family falls ill within weeks of the wedding, so you decide to postpone for six months, if not longer. How much of your money do you get back? What if, when you're ready to reschedule, the DJ doesn't have your new date available? These are things that are out of your control, and things you need to know from your DJ *before* you sign on the dotted line. If you don't like what you hear or read, then this DJ is not for you.

## ❏ *Can I read over your contract before paying a deposit?*

If the DJ says anything but "yes," then avoid a disaster and walk away. There's no reason why a DJ company can't let you read over the contract for your own assurance before signing and putting down a deposit.

## ❏ *How will you prepare for my wedding?*

You'll definitely want to ask them exactly how much time they will spend putting your wedding together. Do they throw it all together at the last minute, or do they go through the details until they know it all by heart?

I once heard a story from a coordinator about a DJ who, first of all, showed up late to the ceremony and then didn't have the song that the bride wanted to walk down the aisle to (a very popular classical piece used at numerous weddings). This DJ should have never let the wedding get this far without knowing every song the bride wanted for not just her ceremony and reception but also for before the ceremony, for cocktail hour, and for dinner music.

When it comes time to submit your music choices to the DJ, *make sure* that they both have the songs and also know the right versions of all the important songs. If your first dance song is a ballad and they end up playing the club mix because that's the only version they have, it's a setup for disaster. I mean, this is your first dance song, the most important song of the night. Verify with your DJ *any* songs that you are using to avoid situations like this. As their client, their number one priority is *you*. *Your* desires, *your* needs, *your* wants, all pertaining to *your* wedding. They work for *you*, not the other way around. Once you do find that DJ that you connect with, then your wedding will be all that it's supposed to be: beautiful and memorable.

### ☐ *What type of setup will you have for my ceremony?*

If you need the DJ to also handle the music for your ceremony, they will need to have some sort of second system, especially if the ceremony is being held outside. For example, what type of mic will they have for your officiant? A lapel mic is always the preferred type because then they can use their hands to freely read from their Bibles, notes, or an iPad, and it's not as noticeable in photos. If you were to poll 100 officiants, 99 percent of them would say that they prefer to use a lapel mic, so make sure your DJ has one. A wireless mic attached to a mic stand at the altar just won't look good in your wedding photos.

Ask what brand of mics the DJ uses, and research it all online. If you know the top-of-the-line models, then you'll know that there shouldn't be any hiccups at your wedding if they're using the best.

I stress this again: Don't be afraid to ask questions. You're not just shopping for a purse or furniture; you're hiring someone to run music on the most romantic day of your life. Don't feel like you're asking too many questions. If a DJ seems annoyed by all the questions you're asking before you hire them, imagine what they'll be like when you need to change a song for the wedding. *Never* apologize for asking more questions or even changing songs on them. It's their job to cater to *you*.

## ❏ *What if you don't have a song that I want?*

This is another great question to ask, in my opinion. In my business, I offer complete control in picking out as many songs as the couple wants, especially the songs for special moments. You need to ask a DJ what happens if they don't have a song that you want included in your wedding. General music that you pick out for basic dancing or playing through the night is one thing, but songs that you've picked out for your formal dances, grand entrance, and tosses are of the utmost importance. For this you need to know two more things:

### ❏ *What if a song I want for my wedding isn't in your library?*

Their answer could be a make-or-break situation for you. If they want *you* to send them the song or songs, move on to the next DJ. They should say nothing other than "I will get it for you."

The other question you need to ask if they answer yes, is:

### ❏ *Where do you get your music from?*

Most couples don't ask me where I get my music from, but I know they also don't want bad quality music. Imagine you're on the dance floor, sharing in your first dance, something that you've envisioned since the day he proposed . . . and the song skips. It skips because it's a bad quality file. I personally get all my music from iTunes because I know that it's good quality; I'm not grabbing a free-off-the-internet file to save a buck. A DJ should never charge you for music that *they* have to obtain for *your* wedding that you hired *them* to handle. You need to be assured that the music they get for your wedding is skip-free and top quality because you can't redo a first dance.

### ❏ Do you have a "do not play" list?

As a DJ, it's impossible to know what songs or artists the couple wants you to avoid playing if they haven't told you explicitly. That's why "do not play" lists are essential. There could be a song that you absolutely don't want in your wedding, a song that maybe you have bad memories about. If there's anything at all that you don't want played, your DJ should respect your wishes.

If you're fine with guests making requests and you've already told the DJ the songs and/or artists you don't want played, his or her next question should be "What if a guest requests it?" This especially holds true for line dances that you may not want played.

### ❏ Do you tape down your cords, and, assuming so, what do you use to do it?

A good DJ will only use gaffer tape when attaching their cords to the floor. Gaffer tape, unlike regular duct tape, is made to hold down cords and cables without leaving ugly residue. Believe me when I say this: Venue owners and management do not like gluey residue left on their floors. They could charge you a fee for it.

If the DJ that you're interviewing says, "Oh, we don't need to tape down our cords," then ask for a photo of their setup. You don't want to be responsible for any guests tripping and falling because the DJ was negligent about their cords. The last thing you need at your wedding is an injured guest because the DJ you hired didn't have sense enough to properly secure their cables and cords.

### ❏ Do you talk over the music?

Let me stress this: A good DJ will not talk over the music. Have you ever noticed how radio DJs talk at the beginning of the song but stop talking once the lyrics kick in? There's a reason for that. Listeners tune in to hear their favorite songs, not to hear the DJ talk all over them. The same applies to weddings. Guests get on the dance floor to dance and groove on whatever song is playing. They don't want to hear the DJ talking all over the music. My philosophy has always been *Say what needs to be said and then let the music play.*

A subquestion here might be "What's your style of DJing?"

You most likely want the vibe to be chill during the dinner with more energy later for the dance floor. No one wants to hear the DJ's thoughts on life while people are eating; that's the time for guests to chat and catch up with each other.

## ❏ *How do you transition between songs?*

Ask the DJ how they will transition from song to song when they're at your wedding. Do they cut off songs if they're not working? Do they cue up music and eliminate long song intros? You may not think it's important right now, but when you get to the dance floor and the DJ lets a few seconds of silence slip in between one song and another, guests will notice, and so will you.

I can't tell you how many times I'd gotten a request for a song from a guest only to see it bomb. Have I ever faded out a song? Quite a few times, especially if it clears the dance floor. Any DJ that says it's never happened to them isn't being honest. In order for the wedding to be considered a success from a DJ's standpoint, the dance floor needs to have people on it. Sometimes a song doesn't get everyone running out there, but a couple of minutes later, dancers do eventually come out. That's why before I do any fading, I at least give it a couple of minutes to see what it does first.

However, the clearing of the dance floor isn't always a bad thing. Sometimes people just need to take a break, sit down, or get a drink. That's usually the cue for the DJ to switch up genres or play something slow until the energy level comes back up.

### ❏ *Do you require to be fed, and do you drink on duty?*

A good DJ won't specify in their contract that they need to get fed. I've never included a clause in my contract that requires the couple to feed me. If they offer, great! If not, I'm not forcing the issue. I can understand the coordinator and the photographer requiring a plate because they're with you the entire day, but the DJ isn't.

If you were to hire a cleaning team to come and deep-clean your home, would you expect something in their contract that says they need to use your kitchen to cook themselves a meal? Of course not. After all, they're only there for a few hours, much like the DJ at your wedding. It's the same scenario if you hire a lawn care service to come to your house and cut your lawn; they certainly don't ask to be given bottles of water or a snack. So why does a DJ need to tell you to feed them if you want their services? If you want to offer food, that's a different story. Most DJs will appreciate the offer. But to demand a meal? No way. Make sure you look over their contract *first* before you sign anything. And before you sign anything, read it over again.

As for drinking on duty, no DJ should ever walk up to the bar and get an alcoholic drink. If he or she wants to be a fun, energetic DJ, then they should be able to do it sober. The same holds true if the party is rocking and one of the guests offers them a beer; they should respect you and your wedding enough to turn it down. If you hire a contractor to build your house, I'm guessing you wouldn't want them popping a top while they're nailing two-by-fours. So if a DJ has to be drinking to have fun at your reception, find someone else. So make sure you ask: *What is your policy on food and alcohol?*

### ❏ *What brand equipment do you use and how much of it will you bring to the venue?*

These are optional questions you can always ask. In a small-to-medium sized room, a DJ does not need to bring everything they own just because they have it, especially if they're positioned in front of the dance floor. Guests know that when open dancing begins, the music will get louder, but if the DJ is concentrating specifically on the dance floor area, then the tables farther away should only be able to hear the music in the background. Not everyone in the room needs to be blasted out.

*Tip: If there are any tables in front of the speakers, a good DJ will go up to the people sitting there and apologize.*

Yes, you read that right. Why is the DJ apologizing? It's just good business. If your DJ happens to be set up in front of any tables rather than in front of the dance floor, the guests will appreciate it so much that they may rave to you about it. "That DJ was so considerate of our feelings." What couple doesn't want to hear sentiments like that?

I was at a wedding not long ago where I was set up directly in front of a few tables where the older guests were seated. In order for the music to stretch toward the other side of the room, I had to keep the volume somewhat high though not yet booming in the early part of the evening. So, I went up to the table directly in front of me and apologized in advance and told them to let me know if the volume needed to be adjusted. One of the guests at that table thanked me for my interest in their comfort and said that it made them happy.

Then there's the dark side: Grandma and Grandpa can't hold conversations because the music is entirely too loud. The DJ brought towering amps and speakers to show off how cool their system is and how loud it can get. After the wedding, Grandma and Grandpa may tell you, "Whoever your DJ was, they were just too loud and obnoxious."

Photo by Pathdoc/Shutterstock, ID 155126723

See the difference?

♪ ♪ ♪ ♪

These questions will help you make good decisions when choosing the right DJ for you. There are so many out there, but once you start throwing questions at them, you'll find a lot of them will fall off your list. Don't choose your DJ only based on their price. Remember, you get what you pay for, and your wedding shouldn't suffer because of it.

# 5

## Booking the DJ

So, YOU'VE FOUND THE **DJ** YOU WANT. Are they over-the-moon excited to be your choice? They should be! The next part, the booking process, should be relatively easy and painless, and you should not feel like you need to consult an attorney to understand their contract. Is it easy to understand? Can you read it over before signing? Don't sign anything until you're 100 percent comfortable with the terms.

Don't just skim through the contract and sign it; read it thoroughly. If the DJ has it in their contract that the venue needs to be made available for setup two hours beforehand but the venue isn't opening their doors until an hour before, you may have a problem. If they demand to be let into the space when they expect to be, well, *you* signed the contract agreeing to it. If their contract stipulates that they need to have a power source within 25 feet of their setup and they get there and the nearest outlet is all the way across the room, they could demand to be moved to where that outlet is, even though that's where you have the cake table. So, read that contract front to back, sideways, and upside down until you know what they expect and what you can deliver. If you're unsure about being able to meet a certain clause in the contract, contact your venue manager and/or coordinator *before* signing anything.

Having been in the business for over 20 years, I've heard horror stories about DJs canceling on a couple, leaving them to fend for themselves to try and find a replacement at the last minute. (I've actually *been* that replacement in a few situations, and they gave me wonderful reviews afterward.) A DJ company should take care of their clients, even when cancelling. It's the little things like that that I'd like to help brides be more aware of.

When I take deposits, they are nonrefundable. By taking the deposit, I am locking in your date. That way no one else can book me on that date, and I won't inadvertently double book myself. It's awkward for a couple if the DJ is trying to rush out of their reception to get to another one. I've had assistants before, but I've never booked more than one wedding a day. As I said in the previous chapter, couples typically want the DJ they interviewed and booked with, not a replacement.

When Hurricane Ike hit in 2008, I'd had a wedding booked in Galveston, Texas, for that fateful weekend. Once the couple rescheduled, I had to decide if I would be willing to drive to their new location five hours away or if I would give them a full refund. I chose to make the drive and fulfill my contract with the couple. Sure, I could've given them a full refund because of what it says in my contract: Where weather is an unforeseen occurrence and rescheduling can't be done in a reasonable amount of time, then yes, a full refund will be given. But, they did reschedule and I wanted to continue to be their DJ, so the travel, although long, was worth it because I fulfilled my obligation to them.

If you're 100 percent comfortable with the DJ you're hiring and are ready to move forward, by all means, get started. Just make sure they've answered all your questions and you're happy with the answers. Once you feel confident and you trust them completely, and you understand the stipulations and everything is good to go, the contract can be signed. Just make sure they're really the DJ you want, because you can't change your mind later on down the road, especially since the rest of the good DJs will probably already be booked for your date.

# 6

---

# Prep and Planning

*N*OW THAT YOU'VE SECURED YOUR **DJ**, IT's time to get into the planning stages. First off: What kind of online planning does your DJ offer? Are you able to log onto a website and utilize a planning form where you can easily add the details of your event, or did they tell you to "just e-mail them" a list of songs and a timeline? The answers to these questions should indicate right off the bat what type of planning you can look forward to—or, not look forward to, as the case may be.

E-mails and texts can get lost or accidentally deleted. What you need is an online system where you can, at your convenience, put in all the details of your wedding. Not to mention, there's so much more to it than just submitting a timeline and some songs, things that any good DJ needs to know. You don't want the DJ to have to ask you every 15 minutes what's happening next or what song you want for the bouquet toss. Online planning is the way to go. That way everything is saved; everything is documented and easily accessible. When couples log on to my website to pick out the music for the formal dances or other events, I get an update almost immediately. If I don't have the song, I make sure I can get it well in advance of the day of the wedding, and if there's more than one version of the song, I make sure to ask the couple for guidance on which version is the correct one.

So, as I've mentioned previously, what if your DJ doesn't have a song or songs you want? This should be their response: "I don't have it, but I'll get it." Any other answer and you should ask for a better one. There are, however, exceptions. You may already have a specific song on your computer and plan to offer it to your DJ because maybe it can't be found anywhere else. Something else to ask: Where are they going to get it? When I don't have a song, my go-to is always iTunes, and I always download the track at the highest bit rate for optimal sound quality.

Back in the '90s, long before I ever thought of being a professional DJ, I went to my brother's wedding in Midland, Texas. His reception was nice, but the DJ was older, only had a small case of CDs, and stayed seated almost the whole time. When my brother and his fiancé had told him what song they wanted for their first dance, he told them he didn't have it and that if they wanted it played, they would have to bring it to him themselves. That DJ started the fire in me and made me want to DJ for weddings. Though, in that DJ's defense, songs were harder to come by in the days before online streaming and downloads; on more than one occasion I have had to order CDs just for one song, or go out to record stores to see what I could find.

At any rate: No couple should have to provide their songs to their DJ *unless* they specifically offer to do so. If the song is otherwise unattainable and the bride says she can send it to me, I am grateful. But in general, couples are paying the DJ to have supply their music, so it's the DJ's job to get it. (Just be mindful *where* your DJ is getting his music. Hopefully it's not from a disreputable or low-quality site.)

Maybe you already know the songs you want to use. Maybe you have a Spotify playlist going, and it's growing every time a song pops into your head. Maybe you have absolutely no idea what songs you want or should choose. *This* is where your DJ comes in.

Recently, a bride sent me an e-mail and asked if I could suggest some good processional songs. I love coaching and educating because I've done this hundreds of times, so you can depend on me to guide you in the right direction. The first thing I need to know when asked a question like this is what style ceremony you will be having. Are you going for the classical Bach/Beethoven/Vivaldi feel where you want the violin, the piano, and the harp? Maybe you love piano instrumentals. Maybe you want a contemporary love song. Knowing these kinds of things helps me help you pick out the right music, because choosing music is like preparing a dish: You have to have the right ingredients or it just won't taste right. I know this because my daughter used to love making me macaroni and cheese; only thing is, she loved to add sugar to the mix. And just like a bad ingredient, wrong songs won't match the vibe.

Years ago, one of my brides wanted this one particular song for her dance with her dad, and I looked high and low for it—on iTunes, on Amazon Music, on every site I could think of—then finally found an old CD on eBay. I was so excited when I got it, just in time for the wedding, and the look on her dad's face when I played the song was priceless and worth every search I had to do to get it. I never used it again, but even if I had, it wouldn't have had the impact it did the first time. But that's what a DJ does: They make moments happen. If you have the right DJ, they will go above and beyond to make your wedding beautiful.

## Final Consultation with Your DJ

One to two weeks prior to the wedding, you and your DJ should schedule a final consultation. Whether it's a face-to-face meeting, a Zoom call, or just a chat over the phone, it's important to have these conversations to make sure they have everything together. If you haven't scheduled one of these, then you're running the risk of having the wrong version of the wrong song played at the wrong time. Sure, these kinds of consultations can be done via e-mail or text, but there's more of a one-on-one connection through voice than there is with typing. If you only told your DJ that you want "Canon in D" for a ceremony song, you still need to let them know what version you want, since there are lots of different arrangements available that include violins, pianos, acoustic guitars, trumpets, harps, and so forth.

If the DJ is also providing music for the ceremony, the two of you should discuss the following issues:

*Where the speaker(s) will be set up.* In my experience, I've found that a speaker sounds better facing the guests, directly in front of the officiant. If the speaker is in the back, the mic receiver has to travel a bit of a distance to get a signal, and it *could* compromise the strength of the signal. You always want the sound *facing* the guests, rather than coming from behind the backs of their heads.

*What background music should be played.* Background music should be discussed, because you want everything to match the vibe of the ceremony. Maybe you're having a purely classical wedding, so you'll want to have classical pieces playing lightly in the background, usually not more than 30 minutes before the start of the ceremony. I always encourage couples to pick out some songs for me to play, but if they don't, I usually play something to match the aura in the room. However, it's always best not to leave it up to your DJ without at least them giving suggestions on what they should play.

*Whether all the songs (and their correct versions) have been verified and approved.* Make *sure* that your DJ has all the right songs needed, regardless of how many songs are being used. Have them send you the songs so that you can hear for yourself if they're the right versions.

*What announcements need to be made, and whether they'll be made by the officiant or the DJ.* Make sure both your officiant and your DJ are on the same page regarding the announcements to be made.

Of course, the reception music needs to be discussed as well as the overall timeline. You should go over everything with your DJ from start to finish, beginning with the ceremony and then on through the last dance and send-off.

I asked Jordan, a bride I worked with recently, what she stressed over the most when she first began her wedding-planning journey:

> I stressed the most over what others would think. In the beginning phases, I spent much time fretting over if our guests will enjoy the caterer we chose, would they think our wedding was too colorful, will our guests like the drinks we offered? Then, at the end, I'm glad my fiancé and I made decisions based off of what we enjoy and the meaning behind them, because then we were able to enjoy all aspects of our day. If you and your partner are having a good time, then your guests will follow in the celebration.

And what excited her?

> Dancing the night away. My husband's family is Italian and they dance to "C'e La Luna" at all big celebrations. It's a fun dance that everyone can participate in. I remember looking forward to being in the center of the dance floor surrounded by our favorite people for that dance. The moment exceeded expectations and was one of my favorite memories captured that night.

A little side note about Jordan's wedding: It was an outdoor event in a beautiful area full of trees with an inside bar and an Airbnb. However, the week leading up to the wedding brought torrential rains that left the grounds saturated. The day of, the sun was out, the puddles had cleared, and it started out as a perfect day for a wedding. The ceremony went off without a hitch, but no sooner than the "I do's" were said did the dark clouds roll in. Before long, the skies opened up and more downpours took place, and for an hour or more, it began to look like it would be a total washout. Luckily, just as soon as the rains came, they left again, and Jordan, her fiancé Sammy, and their families never once stressed over or worried that their wedding would be a rainy disaster. That day, Jordan married her best friend. The weather cleared, and for the rest of the evening, they danced the night away. The moral of the story: Things happen. You will marry your best friend on your big day, and nothing else matters!

Rachel, a bride I worked with in 2019, said just about the same thing:

> I spent so much time, effort, and stress on decor such as centerpieces, table numbers, table settings, etc. Looking back on the day of our wedding, I don't recall memories of those items at all. It was my husband, family, and friends. All of them, laughing, dancing, and enjoying themselves is what I look back on and cherish the most. People tell you the day goes by so fast so not to stress all those little details, and it is the most accurate piece of advice I received!

# 7

---

# Building the Perfect Timeline

*E*VERY VENDOR THAT YOU'LL BE HIRING FOR your wedding has their own favorite timeline. Of course, a coordinator's time-line can be completely different from a DJ's, because they both have very different goals. The coordinator's job is to make sure everything flows smoothly, so their timeline won't always agree with the DJ's, because the DJ's main job is to get people danc-ing without event interruptions. What do I mean by that? For instance, let's say the coordinator has the cake cutting scheduled in between two open dancing sequences, and it's farther down the timeline than where the DJ thinks it should be. The DJ is playing all the hot songs and the dance floor is full, but then the coordinator comes up to the DJ booth and says it's time for the cake cutting. The DJ will be worried that, once you break up the dancing, it may not be as easy to get all those folks back out there again, especially if guests are going to want to sit down and eat some cake.

So, before I explain my own favorite timeline that I usually suggest to couples, let's define the three most important sections of any wedding reception.

1.  Formal Dances. These include the first dance, the parent dances, and any other parent or sibling dances that you may be having in your itinerary. However, they don't have to all be done together (and if you're having more than three, they probably shouldn't be).

2.  Dinner/Cake/Toasts. This area of the timeline is centered around food and drink. In my experience, it's usually best to keep these three events somewhat together.

3.  Open Dancing/Tosses. If you decide to have a bouquet and/or garter toss, it should happen toward the end of the reception, sometime around the open dancing. If there's a lull in the dancing, that's a great time to break away and do those tosses. Of course, if you're not including those in your itinerary, just let the dancing continue.

So those are the three basic sections of a wedding itinerary. Of course there are other events that can be included, such as an anniversary dance, a wedding party dance, or a shoe game, depending on what your desires are. But for the most part, these are the big three.

Now let's explore the details of my favorite timeline, and you can determine for yourself if this might work well for your reception.

## Grand Entrance

This kicks off the reception. It officially says, "The party doesn't start until we walk in!" So regardless of what song you've picked out for your entrance music, you want to make sure everyone is seated, not standing at the bar or standing around chatting, because this is where the energy starts to build.

## First Dance

In my opinion, there's no better time to do your first dance than right after your entrance. Look at it this way: Guests will be watching you once you enter, and their eyes will follow you wherever you go at this point. They're excited to see you! So it makes sense to walk straight into the room and do your first dance then, because later on, it may not be as easy to find a moment to get that dance going. And if you're a traditionalist, the dance floor is meant to be sacred until the couple completes their first dance; in other words, you don't want people out there dancing to "Boot Scootin' Boogie" before you've had your first dance. That special dance between the two of you "christens" the dance floor.

## Dinner

So as I mentioned above, I recommend having the formal dances grouped into one section. So why wouldn't I want to do the parent dances after the first dance? Mainly because if guests have been at your wedding for at least a couple of hours already, they'll be starving. Appetizers of meats and cheeses won't do it for them; they'll be ready for those fajitas or that bacon-wrapped steak. And besides, I have another reason that I like to do the parent dances a bit later. (More on that soon.)

## Cutting the Cake

Here's where different coordinators like to debate. If you're in a time crunch, or even if you're not, I prefer having the cake cutting before the toasts. Once you've done that initial cut, you can then start the toasts while the caterer or venue staff cuts up the rest of the cake for the guests. That way, by the time the toasts have concluded, the cake will be ready to eat. This is especially important if the guests are fired up and ready to dance. You want to move through these events quickly so that the dancing can start. Otherwise, people will begin to get bored, and when they get bored, they start thinking of other things they'd like to do, and those things don't involve being at your wedding.

Some coordinators choose to push the cake cutting later in the night in an effort to keep the older folks around longer. Here's my take on that: You're just delaying the inevitable. Couples can be under the impression that moving the cake cutting back by an hour will encourage folks to stay, and that's partly true. But mostly you're just delaying their desire to leave. Here's the thing: If the guests are being properly entertained, then more often than not, some will actually stay. But if the DJ is playing nothing but hip-hop and Top 40, then you can imagine the grandparents thinking, "Well, I guess the DJ isn't gonna play any of our music." So why would they stay? If they're really not into the music being played, waiting for the cake may not be worth it to them.

## Toasts

As mentioned above, I personally prefer when the toasts happen after the cake cutting, especially if you're pressed for time. While the couple is cutting the cake, guests can visit the bar to refill their drinks and then you can move right into whoever's taking the mic first. A good DJ will have excellent time management when it comes to this. If you're adamant about having as much dance time as possible, you'll want to organize the schedule of events this way.

However, if you've hired a wedding coordinator, they may have other ideas. I'm not saying that coordinators don't know what they're doing, because most of them really do. But like I mentioned before, their job is mainly to keep things moving; they're not really concerned about dance time like the DJ is. In fact, coordinators will mostly be invisible until it's time for the

tosses and the last dance. All that being said, if there's a coordinator on the floor, I let them run the show, regardless of how it
affects the timeline. I can only make big-picture suggestions.

Photo by Ivash Studio/Shutterstock, ID 394327291

If you do plan to go straight into the toasts, make sure the
DJ reminds the guests to go to the bar to get a refill about five
to ten minutes beforehand. And if you've decided to have champagne toasts, make sure the DJ announces that as well so guests
can either get a refill on whatever they're drinking, or have a
glass of champagne, especially if the caterer or the venue staff
is passing out the glasses. Your main goal here is to have everyone seated with a fresh glass before you start the toasts. Guests
should never have to run up to the bar when the first toaster has
the mic because they weren't paying attention to the six messages
about the refills prior.

## Parent Dances

This is where it starts to get good. Your first dance has been com-
pleted, and now dinner is over as well. You've cut the cake and
done the toasts, so this is the perfect time to kick off the parent
dances. I've always started with the father/daughter dance. Nothing against the groom, but this is the moment that both you and
you dad have been dreaming about since the wedding planning

began, so it just makes sense to start here. Then follow up with the mother/son dance, and there won't be a dry eye in the room. Parent dances are just emotional that way.

This leads into opening up the dance floor, which is why I like to schedule the parent dances for after dinner, cake, and toasts.

### Anniversary Dance (optional)

If you're doing an anniversary dance, the best time for it is right after the parent dances and before opening the dance floor. Think of it this way: Guests will be emotional after seeing you dance with your dad and the groom dance with mom, so they're ready to have a meaningful moment dancing with their own spouses. Not to mention, an anniversary dance is a wonderful icebreaker. People tend not to want to jump up onto the dance floor right away, so this is a way to coax them into it.

### Open the Floor

If you've done the anniversary dance, it's time to get the party started. The DJ should play something up-tempo and energetic to keep folks out there dancing. Timeless classics for this part of the night would include "Celebration" by Kool & the Gang, "Get the Party Started" by P!nk, or "Party Rock Anthem" by LMFAO. (I would advise against playing any rap right off the bat; save it for later.)

### The Tosses

The bouquet and garter tosses are funky, sexy, and fun. So why are they usually done an hour or so before the end of the reception? Well, because the older crowd doesn't really care about this event. Sure, some may stick around for it, particularly the grandparents. But for the most part, the older crowd usually will only stay for the formal dances, the dinner, and the cake then are usually gone by this time of the night. But if the music is good, they'll be entertained and will tell you how much they enjoyed your wedding. Regardless, it's just a fact that people get tired and want to go home. Just remember, though: Today you married your best friend. What else should matter?

## Last Dance

This is how you signal to your guests "The party's over, folks, but there's time for one more dance." You decide if you want something classy, something sweet, or something funky—just make it memorable. Another word of advice: Don't have your DJ announce last call right before the last dance, especially if you're wanting to usher people out quickly. Because here's what will happen: You'll have a line of guests waiting at the bar for that last drink, and it will take that much longer to get them out of the building. So, make sure the DJ announces last call about 30 minutes before the end of the reception so that they have time to get *and finish* their drinks before you do the last dance and prepare for your exit.

As I mentioned above, this is just my personally preferred timeline. Your timeline will certainly depend on your preferences for your wedding and how you and/or your coordinator want things done. The outline I've given here is primarily just a guide to give you an idea of how a timeline works. I've seen toasts done before dinner; I've seen dinner served before the first dance; I've played the music for all the formal dances after dinner. It really depends on you and your wedding.

# 8

## Your Playlist

Photo by GraphicsRF.com/Shutterstock, ID 2480199977

*P*ICKING OUT MUSIC FOR YOUR WEDDING MIGHT be some of the most fun you will have throughout the entire planning process. You probably already have a ton of music sitting on your phone or tablet, and now it's time to narrow down the 475-song playlists you already have started.

Please note that your playlist should specifically be the music that you want to *hear and dance to* throughout the evening. It should *not* include the selections you have picked out for your first dance, parent dances, and tosses. Those songs need to be separate so they don't get lost amidst the general playlist.

To make sure everyone has a good time at your reception, you'll want to pick out enough music that appeals to every guest without focusing on one specific type of music.

For instance, a complete playlist would look something like this:

♪ "Tennessee Whiskey"
—Chris Stapleton

♪ "Cupid Shuffle"—Cupid

♪ "Party Up (Up in Here)"
—DMX

♪ "Friends in Low Places"
—Garth Brooks

♪ "Return of the Mack"
—Mark Morrison

♪ "Rock with You"
—Michael Jackson

♪ "Hey Ya!"—Outkast

♪ "Hips Don't Lie"—Shakira

♪ "Man! I Feel Like a
Woman!"—Shania Twain

♪ "Wondering Why"
—The Red Clay Strays

♪ "I Never Lie"—Zach Top

♪ "Dancing Queen"—ABBA

♪ "Livin' on a Prayer"
—Bon Jovi

♪ "Gasolina"—Daddy Yankee

♪ "Dreams"—Fleetwood Mac

♪ "September"
—Earth, Wind & Fire

♪ "Cha-Cha Slide"
—DJ Casper

♪ "Gold Digger"—Kanye West
feat. Jamie Foxx

♪ "Unwritten"
—Natasha Bedingfield

♪ "Freek-a-Leek"
—Petey Pablo

♪ "Wannabe"—Spice Girls

♪ "In Your Love"
—Tyler Childers

♪ "Wobble"—V.I.C.

♪ "Brown Eyed Girl"
—Van Morrison

♪ "I Wanna Dance with
Somebody"
—Whitney Houston

I took these selections from a recent bride's request list, and as you can see, there's a little bit of everything: some country, some danceable pop, some slow-dance songs, and a little bit of rock.

I also like to recommend that my couples create three different playlists: "Love It" (which is their *gotta play* playlist), "Like It" (with songs they like but don't require to be played), and "Hate It" (songs that they want avoided at all costs). A bride I recently worked with gave me 32 "Love It" songs, 48 "Like It" songs, and 10 "Hate It" songs, including Mark Ronson's "Uptown Funk," Miley Cyrus's "Party in the U.S.A.," Chappell Roan's "HOT TO GO!" and "Pink Pony Club," and Pitbull's "Fireball" featuring

John Ryan. Whatever her reasoning was to exclude those, I made sure to grant her wishes (which means I still would not play them even if guests happened to request one). Your DJ should allow you to make as many requests and do-not-play picks as you need to, because the more you request, the more they can get an idea of the kinds of music you as a couple love and also what you think your guests will want to dance to.

So just by glancing at the request list above, it tells me that she's got the three biggest line dances in there, which will come in handy at some point in the evening. There's also some good country songs in there to switch up the genre, because you don't want to wear the dancers out too early. There's also a few songs in there that I could use for cocktail hour if I wanted to try and get some songs scratched off her list earlier in the night.

Photo by Cristi Bucurie/Dreamstime, ID 154428137

Here's another tip: If there are any songs on your playlist that you specifically want saved for dancing, make sure you tell your DJ. I wouldn't play "Tennessee Whiskey" during dinner because I know it's a great slow-dance song that couples will jump on the floor for. That's another reason why you should give your DJ a list of songs that you want primarily for cocktail hour (that is, songs you don't need to be around to hear), songs for dinner, and then songs for dancing. I have a section in my planning form where brides can list anything they want for cocktail hour and for dinner music, and these are usually separate from their dance-floor playlist.

Here's a good recipe for making a playlist:

- Try to limit yourself to 50 to 75 songs in any one playlist;
- Keep separate playlists for cocktail hour and dinner music;
- Create a do-not-play playlist; and
- Discuss with your DJ comparable songs they can use as fillers.

I also give couples the option to submit a Spotify or Apple Music playlist through my online planning area. That way they don't have to go through each song in my library, adding them one by one. It's important that your DJ makes your music planning as easy and stress-free as possible. You already have enough to stress over with the rest of your wedding planning!

Your DJ should also offer a final consultation when you can go over not just the details of the itinerary but also all of the music that you have picked out. This way, you won't have to worry that your DJ is going to drop some Drake in the middle of dinner.

# 9

---

# The Venue and
# the Vendors

$\mathcal{W}$HEN YOU FIRST WALK IN, YOU KNOW it's the place. This is the place where your wedding will be. As you walk along the ballroom floor, you can already envision people dancing, laughing, and having fun. Generally speaking, the venue is the first thing you will book because you need to confirm a facility to have your special day in. So let's explore a few things to consider both before and after booking.

One of the first things to think about it acoustics. Why do I mention this? Because on your wedding night, you don't want the microphones to sound muffled or the music sounding like the speaker is face down, and you definitely also don't want sound bouncing off the walls. You want good sound in your venue. Metal buildings are difficult because of the way the metal itself reverberates, and if your DJ is set up near any windows, the sound will bounce right off the glass and give an unwanted echo all night long. Sure, maybe the venue looks gorgeous on the outside, but if you walk in and you can hear an echo just from your voice alone, then chances are the same thing will happen when the music's playing. That doesn't mean it's a deal breaker, though—a good DJ can work around that in most cases, so don't sweat the small stuff.

And if it is indeed the place that you want your wedding to be, ask about the temperature too. You don't want it to be too hot or too cold for guests from the time they walk in until the time they walk out; you want people to be completely comfortable. I did a wedding not too long ago where, the week prior to their wedding, the air conditioning had gone out. Luckily, it got repaired before the wedding, and the temperature in the building during the event wasn't bad at all. But what if that hadn't happened the week before but the day of? What would the venue have done to ensure that guests wouldn't be sweating themselves to death? Like I said, things happen; after all, the expression "expect the unexpected" exists for a reason. But you still want to know what their policies are.

This isn't the case for all venues, but some will try to coerce you into using one of the DJs that happens to be on their preferred vendor list. "Preferred" usually just means that they want you to use their guy. That's your choice. If you want to bring in your own DJ, that's your prerogative because you're only paying for the space, not their vendor list. But if you research one of their DJs and like what they have to offer, then by all means book them.

I recently asked Christina Muehe, venue manager of The Lyceum in Galveston, Texas, what should brides know when they visit a venue they're considering. Christina says,

> When brides visit a venue, I see that they are so excited to book
> a place for their dream day that they don't ask before the tour

about the pricing on venue and the hours of rental. I feel like sometimes I tour couples and their families, and then they end up not booking based on budget. As a venue director, I don't mind showing the venues, but it costs time and energy to show the venue, and I feel that couples really should ask the important questions like how long can they have the venue and like pricing, because everyone has a budget.

She continues, "When brides visit the venue, they don't typically have a vision of their day, time frame, how many guests." Christina also says that if brides, after they get engaged, would think about what they want their special day to look like and *then* go to the venues to tour, it would be so much more helpful so that the venue directors can give them better pointers.

She also has tips for day-of coordinators: "Brides should be aware that booking a venue doesn't mean you're also booking a day-of coordinator. They should book them in addition. The venue's staff and directors aren't coordinators; we just manage the venue."

Another important question to ask at the venue, not just for your DJ but for the other vendors as well, is how early will the venue be made available to them? Personally, it takes me *at the very least* an hour and a half to completely set up my system for the reception, not to mention if I need to coordinate sound for the ceremony and then do sound checks.

And as mentioned previously, you should also ask the venue if the lights can be dimmed when dancing begins. If they can't, then you'll know that paying for additional lighting through your DJ will just be a waste of money.

## The Coordinator

In building on what Christina says about choosing the venue, she also wants brides to know that whoever you hire to be your day-of coordinator should have good reviews, referrals, and credentials. They should also always be present at any showings, follow-ups, and rehearsals.

> The bride should not have to make any decisions the day of her wedding. Because if she has a qualified and skilled day-of coordinator, the decisions should be made easy for the bride, and she should have a nonstressful day and relish in it.

I asked Courtney, a seasoned coordinator skilled in the art of running a wedding, what made her decide to get into the wedding coordinator business in the first place, and what she loves about it:

> After my first wedding in 2018, I fell in love with the world of weddings. I realized that if I took my love for weddings and hopeless-romance movies and combined that with new and inventive ways to ease the stress of planning it all, then maybe my business could make it. Little did I know that years later, I would be consistently loving on couples and helping them achieve the wedding of their dreams without pulling out their hair. I genuinely love when couples say right before their wedding: "People ask me if I'm stressed and I give them my honest answer: No, I have Court!" It is truly a blessing to be able to celebrate love every day. By no means is it easy, and bridal fires are real, but the love is worth it. Every single time.

I also asked Courtney what is the one thing that she wishes brides knew before booking *any* vendors.

> Set a budget and stop taking reviews so literally. This is the worst part of the process, because you have to bring your dreams to a realistic level and have an honest conversation about what you can expect and afford. In addition, we live in a "cancel culture." Brides have tons of emotions; this comes with the territory. Take time to read reviews but also understand that a lack of communication or setting clear expectations can

be the main reason why a bad review exists. Be sure to take the time to write out a list of questions you want to ask the vendors but also meet with them face to face—even if it's just on Zoom. Have a real interaction, share your honest thoughts, and decide if that particular vendor will match the energy you are bringing to your wedding day.

About the ceremony Courtney says:

This is honestly my secret sauce; I live and breathe a perfect ceremony. My best advice is to hire a day-of coordinator at minimum and let them run it. If you try to wing this, it's guaranteed that something will be miscommunicated. Coordinators can cue people, open and close the doors at the right time, and even cue the DJ for the next song to play. Having someone who is a third-party vendor can be extremely helpful with this particular part of a wedding day.

Photo by Oliveromg/Shutterstock, ID 151827812

I've personally worked with great coordinators like Court, bad ones, and all the ones in between. There are ones who will be by your side from engagement to the after-party, and then there are ones who are just day-of. In the beginning of my DJ career, I didn't like coordinators because I liked having control of the timeline. But then I realized how much work the coordinator can take off of me when they're doing their job right.

I was at a wedding recently, and it was getting late in the evening, and we hadn't done the formal dances yet. The day-of coordinator was sitting down chatting with guests, the dance floor was empty, and the crowd needed something to happen or else they would start leaving. So, I took matters into my own hands (which is generally the DJ's job anyway when no coordinator has been hired). I announced that the formal dances would be coming up shortly. That announcement let guests know what was coming next so they weren't sitting there thinking that nothing else exciting would be happening. Good coordinators will quite often check in with the DJ to let them know what's next on the timeline so that everyone's on the same page. That being said, the coordinator is as only good as his or her DJ is; it's imperative that they work together as a team to get through the timeline without bothering the happy couple. That's you've hired us: to handle things. Does the DJ have to take the reins sometimes when the coordinator hasn't? Of course. But between the two of them, they should be able to make all the dances and events transition beautifully.

As I've mentioned, usually about a week prior to the wedding, I always made sure to have a final consultation with my couples to go over everything: the dances, the timeline, the events, the dinner, the tosses, the start time, the end time, things like that. And whenever possible, I like to get the coordinator on a conference call as well so that everyone is on the same page. You don't want any day-of surprises, such as the DJ thinking the first dance is before dinner yet the coordinator has it in a completely different slot on her timeline.

Another job of the coordinator is coordinating the wedding ceremony. As a DJ, it helps me immensely to have the coordinator (or their assistants) standing in the doorway and able to make eye contact with me before giving a thumbs-up on when to start the songs. Couples pick out specific songs so that they can walk out to those songs, and if the coordinator isn't sending those people out on *that* song, then chances are, the song will have to be repeated.

For instance, let's say the bridesmaids and groomsmen are coming out to "Speechless" by Dan + Shay. Even though the song is more than four minutes long, if the wedding party doesn't start walking on cue, depending upon how many people there are, the song may have to be repeated. The length of the aisle can be a factor as well. But that's not necessarily a problem, because there have been plenty of times when I've had to reloop a song because it ended, and it's not necessarily anyone's fault. A good DJ can transition the repeats smoothly and without anyone noticing.

If you aren't hiring a coordinator, then the DJ and/or photographer runs the show. If there's a coordinator on the floor, the DJ follows their lead and shouldn't have to make decisions on when things are to be done. For instance, I recently worked a wedding where I saw the coordinator from the ceremony until dinner, and then I rarely saw her until the end. Where did she disappear to? Make sure your coordinator is *on top of things from start to finish*. At another wedding there was a slight error made by a coordinator that I worked with; the guests were supposed to hang out outside of the ballroom rather than going in and finding their seats. There were finger foods outside for them to have, yet that particular coordinator only brought it to my attention after guests had already moved inside. My thoughts are that the officiant, when making the announcement, should have gotten that info from the coordinator *before* the ceremony even started so that the guests would have been directed there in the first place. That coordinator had asked me to make an announcement to usher guests outside, but that didn't really help the guests who were still coming in. So some guests were outside and some were inside. Mistakes happen and they won't ruin the wedding, but *communication is key.*

## The Photographer

Photo by Protsenko_Photo/Shutterstock, ID 569157358

Like the DJ, the photographer is important to the success of the wedding but for completely different reasons. The music can be spot-on, but if photo ops are missed, it can really dampen the bride's spirits. So photographers need to be clued into the order of events just as much as any other vendor. It's always good practice for either the coordinator and/or the DJ to share the timeline with them so that they're not left in the dark at the reception.

I asked Joe Lewis, a wedding photographer in Buffalo, New York, what advice he could give to brides searching for their photo vendor, and what he wishes every bride knew:

> My advice as a photographer to a bride planning a wedding is to loosen up on the itineraries and to understand that no wedding day goes as planned. Expect the unexpected and trust the professionals.

Don't cheap out. Wedding photos are all that's left at the end of the night, aside from the memories. A wedding photographer also aids in making sure everything goes according to plan; they're not just taking photos.

Be prompt. You may have to select photos for an album or package. Don't put it off for months.

Give your maid of honor some duties to help out, like fixing dresses and hair.

Ease up on the drinking before photos—there's plenty of time for that later! Also, ease up on the reception activities, and keep it light; your guests mostly want food, drinks, and dancing.

Understand that "mood" shows up in photos! Be happy, slow down, take it all in, and have a ton of fun!

When I was working as a DJ assistant before I started my own business, there was one time the main DJ announced the first dance and the couple was raring to go. The only problem was that the photographer was in the restroom. Needless to say, that photographer was not happy when he returned to the ballroom to find the couple wrapping up their dance. With every wedding, I learned something new, and this was a great lesson: always make an announcement before a specific event is about to begin. For example, if I'm doing the first dance at 7 p.m., by 6:50 I'm letting the room know what's coming up so no one is caught off guard and unprepared. Same way with the cake cutting, the toasts, the tosses, anything that will capture attention.

On the other side of the token, a photographer should alert the DJ when they're planning to take the couple out of the room for, say, sunset photos on the deck or a few last-minute shots by the gazebo—really, anytime they're being taken away. So many times I would be about to announce something that involved the couple, only to find out that they were outside somewhere taking photos. That may be something you want to mention to both your DJ and your photographer, to keep each other in the loop for upcoming events, whether it's a parent dance or sunset pics. Believe me, you don't want any hiccups that could have otherwise been prevented. When vendors work together, the wedding is a success.

## The Officiant

I was working a wedding in 2015, and I'd just finished setting up the sound system when I heard some rumblings that the officiant hadn't arrived yet. As the start of the ceremony drew closer, everyone was starting to get nervous. You could clearly tell the bride was beyond stressed, and there was just that negative aura that seemed to surround everyone; the last thing anyone wanted was to have to postpone or cancel the wedding. Luckily, the officiant showed up late, and the wedding continued as planned. But it got me to thinking: What would happen if the officiant didn't show up at all? What if, God forbid, there was a traffic mishap or they'd happened to fall ill? Would the wedding have to be rescheduled for another day? And what about the guests who'd had to travel far distances to get to the wedding?

Photo by Virrage Images/Shutterstock, ID 262863614

A few months later, I did an online search for "how to be an officiant," and in 2016, I got ordained. Then I just needed to learn how to officiate a wedding. Even though I'd gotten the license so I could do it in case of an emergency, I wanted to get out there and really learn the craft. I officiated my first wedding a few months later! I learned how to put together a ceremony, I researched scripts, and I finally included my officiant services as an add-on to any wedding package that I offered. (The hard part was figuring out how I would officiate *and* DJ at the same time. Enter Bluetooth.)

When hiring your officiant, ask about a backup *just in case*, because you just never know what might happen. If they don't offer one, inquire with a friend or family member to see if they can act as a backup and would be willing to get ordained.

So, assuming that your officiant, whoever that may be, arrives on time, it's important that you put the DJ and the officiant in touch with each other no later than 30 minutes prior to the start of the ceremony so that the officiant can get mic'd up. If you've hired a coordinator, then it's their job to handle that communication or to delegate it to someone in your wedding party. The important thing is to ensure that both the DJ and the officiant are on the same page.

That's why you hire professionals: to handle things so you don't have to. Your only job should be having the best day of your life.

And speaking of professional advice, here's a quick tip: During the ceremony, be sure to face each other, not the officiant. (Every good officiant should know this too.) Your guests don't want to see the back of your heads; they want to see your smiling faces. And besides, in this moment, you should be looking into each other's eyes anyway.

Then, either the DJ or the officiant should make some additional announcements that will ensure a smooth ceremony:

*Telling everyone to silence their devices before the ceremony begins.* An optional no-pictures-during-the-ceremony announcement can be made at this time as well. These announcements can be made either before the processional walk begins or right before the song starts. I've done weddings where the officiant will walk up to the aisle alone without any music playing to let the guests know to silence their phones. You definitely don't want phones going off in the middle of the ceremony, and you absolutely don't want people jumping in the aisle to take pictures and interfering with the photographer that you paid to take pictures.

*Inviting everyone to "stand as you are able" as you walk down the aisle.* Most guests will automatically stand when they see you coming, but you may want to ask your officiant to make sure people are called to stand as you enter the aisle. It just makes for a nice picture.

*Announcing you as the new mister and missus.* You'd be surprised how many officiants neglect to make this simple but important announcement; so often I've been left standing by, just waiting for the officiant to cue me to start the music by announcing, "Introducing for the first time . . ." So if that announcement doesn't come, I just go ahead and play the recessional song. So make sure of two things: that your officiant moves out of the way for the first kiss for photos and that they announce you how you want to be announced.

*Informing guests where they need to go after the ceremony.* Either the officiant or the DJ can make this announcement, letting everyone know about cocktail hour, when and if the bar is opening, signing the guest book, and anything else that's happening after the ceremony. You'll also want someone to ask the wedding party and immediate family to stick around for photos so they don't go running off somewhere.

## The Caterer

To give more insight into the caterer's side of weddings, I consulted Todd Schott, owner of Chopin Mon Ami catering and director of the Galveston Trolley Station. I asked him to share some things about what you should know before booking a caterer, what you definitely need (even if you don't know it yet), and what to beware of.

Before booking a caterer, a couple should know what their budget is and what type of hors d'oeuvres and entrées they would like to serve. Most clients getting married have no idea what caterers charge, what services they perform, and what gratuities are charged. For instance, when a caterer charges a price per person for hors d'oeuvres, how many of those are being supplied? What size portion are the hors d'oeuvres? Also, with the entrée. What are the portion sizes for the cost? Does the client really need four hors d'oeuvres for cocktail hour? Is four hors d'oeuvres too many for the size of the entrée that's being served? Is the caterer taking advantage of the client to sell more to the client? So, the client needs to relate their expectations to the caterer and identify if the caterer can meet the client's expectations.

Your DJ also needs to be somewhat aware of what's going on with the caterer. There have been times I've followed a coordinator's timeline to the letter, only to find out, after announcing that dinner is ready, it's really not. A DJ needs to have their eyes all over the room; they're often in the unique position to know what's happening or not happening before anyone else. One of the things they can help with is going up to the caterer before the wedding party even enters to find out when dinner will be ready. If dinner service is scheduled for right after the grand entrance but the food isn't ready, you'll just be wasting precious time. You definitely don't want to have someone come up and take the mic to do a special blessing, only for the room to then be filled with dead air afterward because dinner isn't ready yet.

I've worked lots of weddings where I introduced the wedding party but also knew that dinner service wouldn't be ready just yet. So I would say something like, "Dinner service will begin shortly, so in the meantime, visit the bar, mingle, and chat, then sit back, relax, and enjoy the music." By making this type of announcement, guests are kept in the loop. Otherwise, they're clueless and thinking, *Should I go smoke? Should I go to the restroom? What's happening next?*

In my opinion, all vendors should work as *one team* and for *one reason*: to ensure that your wedding day runs as smoothly as a chocolate fountain in the summer.

## The Bartender

Let's hear a bit more from Todd, this time with his expert advice on bartending services:

Before booking a bartender find out: Are they certified? Do they know how to make drinks that the clients want to serve? The rule of thumb is one bartender per 100 guests. If you are serving a full bar or complicated drinks that require more time to mix, you might want to add another bartender. For a wedding, how much liquor, beer and wine do you need to buy? I use the method of five drinks per person for a four-hour reception. 100 people would be 500 drinks; 250 liquor drinks and 250 beer and wines. You get 28 shots of liquor out of a liter. So, divide 250 by 28 and that gives you your 9 liters of liquor you would need to buy. To learn how much beer and wine you need, take the 250 and divide by 2, and this gives you 125 beers and 125 glasses of wine; beer is 24 bottles per case. So, to get the correct number of beers for the reception, 125 beers divided by 24 gives you 5.2 cases of beer to buy. If you need to serve 125 glasses of wine, divide 125 by 5 glasses of wine to get the number of bottles of wine you would need. This gives you 25 bottles of wine. If your crowd is a heavy-drinking crowd, you might want to do six drinks per person for a four-hour reception. Keep in mind that a wedding reception is a celebration, *not* a frat party!

A DJ and an open bar work hand in hand for the overall success of the party. After all, the bar will be the first place wedding guests visit following the ceremony and the final place they visit once the last call is announced. However, alcohol can get pricey.

From my experience, most couples elect to just offer beer, wine, soda, and water at their open bar, though some bring in a margarita machine and others will have champagne on hand for the special toasts. Everything boils down to budget.

I do know this: Guests love an open bar, not so much a cash bar. Ninety-five percent of the time, weddings that I've worked have had an open bar, just because brides want their guests to have a good time and to eat, drink, and be merry. The few times that I've seen a cash bar, not a lot of people will visit it unless they really need a drink.

And what makes a happy bartender? Tips, especially when a DJ *reminds* guests to tip. When I'm announcing that the toasts are happening in a few minutes, I always remind guests to tip their bartender. First of all, they appreciate that sentiment because they know the DJ is looking out for his fellow vendor. And second, the DJ won't be sending people over there all at once. The only other time that I announce anything regarding the bartender is at last call, usually 30 minutes prior to the last dance and/or grand exit (or send-off). No bartender wants guests staggering up to the bar when they're trying to shut everything down. Like the other vendors, they are excited to be a part of your day, but after a long evening filled with magic and memories, they're ready to punch out.

The only other thing I would ask before hiring your bartender is if they look out for inebriated guests. You don't want your bartender continuing to pour drink after drink for Uncle Bob who loves those whiskey shots. If one of your guests is totally blasted, you want to make sure they get home, or to their hotel or wherever they're staying, safe. The bartender can confiscate their keys and get them an Uber. Even better, let your guests know you'll be offering those services to anyone who may need help without asking for it; hand out little certificates that guests can use. The fact that you care enough about their well-being to make sure they get home safe might mean more to them than the actual invite to your wedding. After all, with an open bar the old slogan goes: The open bar is on you, but the hangover is on them.

# 10

——

# Planning the Ceremony

*Y*OU DREAMED OF THIS AS A LITTLE girl, exactly how it would go. You envisioned it, and now the time is getting close. All of your dreams will be put into action. So much thought and planning goes into a ceremony that lasts usually no more than 30 minutes.

## The Wedding Rehearsal

Most couples think that the DJ needs to be present at the rehearsal, but they don't. Your officiant doesn't need to be there either. All you're doing is practicing the walk, and this can be done without music. Both the DJ and the officiant will charge you extra for their appearance when it's not needed, regardless of what coordinators may think. A good DJ will know when to start and end the music (and in some cases, when to reloop). The only thing your officiant will do when they get to the rehearsal is walk; there's no need to go over the script, because that's something they should go over with you in private well before the rehearsal is scheduled.

Photo by Nicoleta Ionescu/Shutterstock, ID 296444204

The only vendor that needs to be present for your rehearsal is your coordinator, if you've hired one, or whoever else will be in charge of the lineup and the walk because they'll be largely responsible for making sure each group starts on the song that you've picked out. It's that person's job to become familiar with every song being used not just for your ceremony but for your reception, too.

## Planning the Procession

There are really two traditional ways of deciding who's walking and when.

The first way:
- Officiant, groom, and best man;
- Parents and grandparents;
- Bridesmaids escorted by groomsmen;
- Maid or matron of honor;
- Flower girl(s) and ring bearer(s);
- Bride.

The alternate:
- Officiant and groom;
- Best man and groomsmen (from the side);
- Parents and grandparents;
- Bridesmaids (from the front);
- Maid or matron of honor (from the front);
- Flower girl(s) and/or ring bearer(s);
- Bride.

When deciding on the procession, you have to discuss with your coordinator, or whoever else may be overseeing the ceremony, what works best for you. There's no set way or order that need to be followed.

## Prelude: Background Music and Announcements

Background music is just nice, calming music played softly while guests find their seats in the 30 minutes prior to the ceremony. You should be able to select some songs to have played, or at least set the mood and vibe with your DJ, but it shouldn't be anything you'd want played at the reception for dancing, e.g, "Uptown Funk," "Party Rock Anthem," "Get Low," etc. Classical pieces, instrumentals, and ballads all work beautifully, but your choices might also can depend on what you've chosen for your walk. If you've picked "Canon in D" for your walk or the bridal party's, music from artists like Vitamin String Quartet or Brooklyn Duo work great. If your DJ is experienced, then they should know what will work best but make sure you have some input. If there are songs that you want played in the background, those requests should be granted, regardless of what the DJ wants to play.

I've always had a pet peeve when it comes to the ceremony: Do you start on time, regardless of whether or not guests are still showing up, or do you delay it to accommodate the latecomers? My take is that both guests and vendors are well aware of when your wedding is slated to start, so you shouldn't have to delay *your wedding* because they can't get there on schedule. I've seen it too many times. It's just disrespectful in my opinion, and it puts your entire itinerary behind. But, ultimately, the decision is yours.

Wedding guests also need direction. They need to know what's next and where to go. There are two people responsible for making announcements about the ceremony: the officiant and the DJ.

Before the ceremony starts, you should have someone announce, and reiterate many times, that phones need to be silenced. Someone's ringtone going off in the middle of the ceremony throws everybody off and just ruins the atmosphere. It won't hurt your guests to silence their devices for 30 minutes.

Another thing to consider is courtesy regarding informal photos. I was DJing a wedding once where I saw a guest jump into the aisle to take a picture of the couple while the photographer the couple paid good money for was set up right behind this guy. Guests need to know that you're pay the photographer to take photos, so they need to be mindful not to get into the way. So that's the other announcement that I typically will make, especially if the officiant doesn't. If you don't let people know your desires, they won't respect them. It's pretty simple: Silence your phones, and let the photographers do their job.

Another announcement that either the officiant or the DJ can make during the ceremony is for guests to rise as you come down the aisle. Most people do it automatically, but if they don't, it's nice to announce that they should. It's just a nice respect thing for you as the bride.

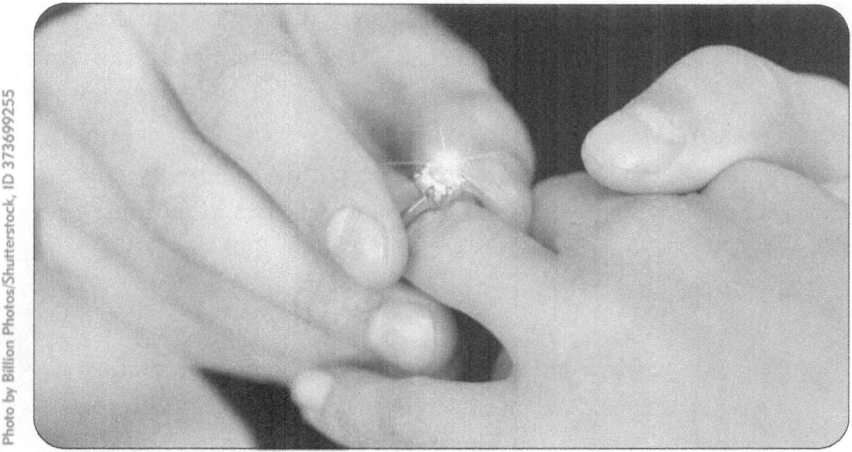

## Ceremony Songs

For the ceremony itself, you'll need to pick between one and four songs, depending on what you have planned:

- Groom's entrance song;
- Seating of the mothers (if separate from groom's entrance);
- Bridal party;
- Flower girl(s) and/or ring bearer(s) (if separate from the bridal party's entrance);
- Your entrance (which is called the processional);
- Your exit as newlyweds (which is called the recessional).
- You can combine certain songs, like the bridal party's song if the walk isn't very long, but I would have your own song to walk out to, just for the emotion alone. Having your own song indicates that you've entered the ceremony.

A lot of brides will send me YouTube links for songs that they want to use either for the bridal party's walk or their own walk, which I'm always fine with, but keep in mind that not every DJ will be able to use those links unless they have a program that converts the video into an audio file that can be played without ads. If possible, try to find that exact song on iTunes if you can.

If you can't source it there, be sure to see if your DJ can convert a YouTube link, and then make sure to request a copy of the converted file so that you know you're happy with the way it sounds. Any DJ should be more than willing to go above and beyond to get you the songs you want for your ceremony. There are always cases where the song you want for your walk can't be found anywhere, as was the case with Nick and Kylie's wedding.

Nick explains:

I had the privilege of playing a recording of my grandfather singing "Al Señor yo le quiero servir," a song that holds a deeply special place in my heart. This song means the world to me for many reasons, but most of all because it reminds me of the man who taught me how to live with integrity, courage, and a heart devoted to serving others. My grandfather showed me what it means to be a good man: honest, selfless, and unafraid to stand firm in his beliefs.

As I walked to the altar, I could feel his voice beside me, not just through the music, but in spirit. Though he is no longer with us, having his voice guide me in that moment was more than symbolic; it was sacred. It was a quiet promise to the man whose name I proudly carry, a vow that the same love and strength he lived by will now be the foundation I build my marriage on. I carry his legacy forward, not only in name, but in action, as a message to my wife and to my family of the kind of husband—and man—I strive to be.

Kylie sent me an audio file, and I was easily able to convert it to play at the wedding; I also sent them the finished product beforehand to make sure they were happy with it. Songs like this are special to the couple and to the family, and every DJ should be excited to play something like that. As the song filtered through the speaker, I glanced over at Nick's dad, who had tears in his eyes. It's moments like those that I'm honored to be a part of as a DJ.

Photo by Shutterstock AI, ID 2630078879

## Here Comes the Bride

I had a past bride ask me once, "Do I have to stand there at the altar with my dad until the song is over?" I really couldn't believe that a DJ *wouldn't* fade out the entrance song as they arrive at the altar, but nothing in this business surprises me anymore based on what I've heard other DJs do and not do. Rest assured, I've *always* faded out the processional music right before the officiant says "Who gives this woman . . ." But, it's worth checking to ensure that your DJ will fade out your entrance song because, believe me, you don't want to have to stand there awkwardly for two and a half minutes, and I'm sure your officiant doesn't want to either.

There are a couple of other things that your DJ should be prepared to do: Reloop any song during your ceremony should it end too soon and edit your recessional song. If I had a nickel for every time I had to reloop a song because it was about to end before the last wedding party member got to their position at the altar, I'd be rich. Your DJ needs to be ready to do the same, because you definitely don't want any dead air during your ceremony, and if your DJ is good, they should be able to seamlessly transition from the end of the song back around to the beginning without any break in the music.

The other thing your DJ should do, and they should probably do it before the wedding, is edit your recessional song. Let's say you picked a song that has a long intro but the good part of the song is after the two-minute mark. You can have your DJ edit the track to a specific start and/or end time, and they should be able to accommodate your request. In fact, once you choose your recessional song, decide in advance where you want the song to start so you know exactly where the song will begin after you are pronounced husband and wife.

## Special Additions

Photo by Peter Istvan/Shutterstock, ID 442518310

There are so many rituals and special moments that you can add to your ceremony such as:

- A salt or sand ceremony;
- A dove or butterfly release;

- Hand-tying;
- Jumping the broom;
- Glass breaking;
- Wedding branding

Some of these rituals are done during the ceremony and some are done after, but any of them can have a specific song played lightly in the background, with the exception of the glass-breaking and jumping-the-broom rituals that are typically done at the end of the ceremony.

## A Special Touch: Love Letters

Photo by Sergii Sobolevskyi/Shutterstock, ID 1144533248

A nice gesture that no one has to be involved with other than you and your fiancé is to write each other love letters before the ceremony starts. I can't stress enough how important it is to focus on each other in this moment, rather than wondering if the DJ is set up, if the photographer is in place, or if the guests are in their seats. What is most important, above all else, is that today you are marrying your best friend.

Should you still write love letters to each other even if you've written your own vows to each other for the ceremony? Of course! These letters don't have to be anything more than a simple sentiment or a quick note; just write what you're feeling at that moment. The vows that you read to each other at the wedding will represent your past, your present, and your future; they most likely won't reflect the moments you're experiencing just minutes before that first song of the ceremony begins playing. And these love letters can be something that you can always look back on and remember those minutes before your "I do's."

Are you a crier? If you think you aren't, believe me when I say that on your wedding day the tears will flow, but they'll of course be happy tears. The atmosphere, the sunshine, the smell of the flowers, and the taste of the wine are all leading up to the moment when you marry your best friend. Don't worry if your makeup will smear or your mascara will run. Write that love letter and have it delivered by your maid of honor. When you write those words you're feeling, you won't believe the amount of stress that leaves you.

## Introducing the New Mister and Missus

Photo by Monkey Business Images/Shutterstock, ID 345831998

The recessional song is the one song that doesn't have to absolutely match the style of the other songs you have picked out for the ceremony. It's the song that says, "We're married, let's party!" So you want to pick out something that has *fun* written all over it, but again, avoid picking out something that you might want played later on during the reception for dance time.

Remember, this is *your* ceremony so you should tailor it to your personality. It all goes by so quickly, but these moments will be remembered in photos for the rest of your lives together.

## Postceremony Announcements

After the ceremony, guests need to know: Do we sit here and wait? Do we get up and get a drink? Find our seats? Sign the guest book? Either your officiant or your DJ should make an announcement like, "This concludes the ceremony. Guests may now head inside, grab a drink, and find your seats. Wedding party and immediate family, please stay behind for photos with the newlyweds." By making this announcement, guests are directed to the cocktail hour (and/or to grab some appetizers if you're offering that). It also instructs the family and wedding party not to go off somewhere but to instead stay somewhere close for photos. This also helps the photographer because then they don't need to look all over the grounds for them.

Getting through the ceremony will probably be the most stressful part of the whole wedding, just because you want everything to be perfect. But what is perfect? You're getting married under sunny skies, and you're marrying your best friend. That alone is a perfect day. Songs skipping, an empty dance floor, people leaving early, mics not working? That's all water under the bridge and out of your control. Things happen, but you should focus on why you're there in the first place: You're marrying your best friend.

# 11

---

# Wedding Bell Blues

$\mathcal{P}$LANNING AND LIVING YOUR WEDDING DAY CAN come with its share of ups and downs, from last-minute hiccups to nerves that tend to sneak up just as you're about to walk down the aisle. But those wedding bell blues are a totally normal part of the journey. But here's the good news: With a little preparation, some deep breaths, and the right mind-set, you can turn those moments of stress into memories of calmness, joy, and laughter. This chapter is all about helping you navigate the emotional rollercoaster of your big day so you can focus on what really matters: celebrating your love.

Caleb remembers his wedding day very well:

> Honestly, I wasn't really nervous about much. For me, the day
> started off great with the alcohol and my boys with me that

helped calm my nerves for the day, so it wasn't too bad. I was a little nervous at the altar but only because my bride looked so beautiful! If I had to give one thing, though, it would be that I was nervous about other people ruining the day for my wife, whether it be family drama or someone arguing or just people getting drunk. My wife spent a lot of time planning and building for six hours of one day. So I was on edge for it to be perfect and everything she had dreamed of.

## Blame It on the Rain

Photo by Steve Lovegrove/Shutterstock, ID 78142960

It's been pouring all morning, and you don't know if it's going to let up long enough to have your much anticipated wedding outside in the sunshine. The chairs are getting wet; no one can go out there to decorate; it's a mess. I get it. I know what you're feeling, especially if you have to go to plan B. Unfortunately, we can't control the weather, and there's always a chance that it could rain on your wedding day. Some say it's good luck, but that's not what you're thinking when the dark skies are rolling in. You will need to make some difficult decisions.

A DJ won't set up in the rain. Their first priority is to protect their equipment from weather hazards, so it's up to you to make the call and to let the DJ know your plans. At the very least, designate a go-to person that will keep them informed and updated on what's happening, especially because some DJs don't have easy setups for an outside ceremony. DJs need enough time to get themselves out there, get the equipment out there, plug everything in, check the music levels, and check the mic levels. So believe me, they are watching the weather just as much as you are, if not more. So be sure you keep your DJ in the loop on what your plans are currently and in the immediate future.

Hiccups at a wedding are expected. Sometimes a boutonniere might go missing, a song cue gets delayed, or the flower girl suddenly decides the aisle is a racetrack. These little mishaps don't ruin the day and can often become the moments you laugh about later. Your guests won't remember that the cake was served ten minutes late, but they *will* remember the joy, love, and energy that filled the room. A wedding isn't perfect because everything goes exactly according to plan; it's perfect because you're marrying the love of your life. The rest is just background noise.

# 12

---

# Cocktail Hour

Photo by Andreblais/Dreamstime, ID 5862049

THE COCKTAIL HOUR, OTHERWISE KNOWN AS THE thing that happens in between the ceremony and the party, which can be held in a separate room, inside the ballroom, or on the patio, is an hour's worth of mingling, drinks, and appetizers. It's also the time for the DJ to start entertaining the crowd, not necessarily with dance music but to create more of a toe-tappin' atmosphere with feel-good songs that will put a fun vibe out there. What the DJ plays during this time will give the guests a preview of what they can expect later in the evening, but you'll generally want to avoid any rap or hip-hop that might not fit in. The music also doesn't need to be loud; it's purely background music for guests to enjoy, so make sure you relay that with your DJ as well, to keep it low and subtle. I always give my couples the option to pick out an hour's worth of music that they want me to play during this time, but even if they don't, I pretty much have free rein on entertaining the crowd. Motown tracks work well here, as does country, classic rock, and crooners like Frank Sinatra, Dean Martin, and Bobby Darin.

If you do decide to pick out specific music to have the DJ play during cocktail hour, just keep in mind that you won't be able to hear any of those songs since you'll probably still be with the wedding party taking photos. Just make sure that your DJ doesn't play something that you want saved for later if they choose any songs from your playlist. Though if they've been doing this for a while, they should know what to play and what to save.

Cocktail hour usually doesn't call for many announcements from the DJ, other than basic reminders to sign the guest book, to fill out advice cards, and to find their seats along with anything else that might need relaying. However, during this time, I always walk the room to see if there is anything else that I can mention, such as:

- Disposable cameras on the tables for guest use;
- Candy bars for the kiddos;
- Photo booth operating hours;
- Caricature artist operating hours; and
- Any other special things that are set up for guest use.

For example, I've seen tables with a special retro telephone that guests can pick up to leave special audio messages for the couple. There is no shortage of how many ideas can come forth for entertaining your guests, and the DJ needs to pay special attention to those.

Some DJs will go around to the tables, introducing themselves and making small talk and maybe even taking a few early requests. It's always great when DJs interact with the guests, to feel them out and to get an idea of what the crowd might enjoy hearing throughout the night. But as your big entrance gets closer, the DJ will need to get on the mic and ask guests to find their seats. This should happen five or ten minutes before you're ready to walk in, whether that's with or without your wedding party. You don't want a line of people at the bar getting drinks or standing in your path between the doors and the dance floor when the music starts pumping. Everyone needs to be in their seats and ready to scream and shout for your big entrance.

# 13

---

# The Grand Entrance

*F*INALLY IT'S TIME THE MUCH AWAITED, MUCH anticipated grand entrance, the true start of the party. High energy is needed for this, because this is what gets the party started.

## First, Take a Breather

Before you get announced, take five or ten minutes alone together to take it all in. This is a moment to renew and refresh. Have a glass of wine, look around, and just breathe, because it will go by so fast, and you'll feel like you're being pulled in every direction at every minute. You'll feel rushed all night, but this is a time when you can put the brakes on for just a bit. That'll give you a second wind, enough energy to get ready to have the time of your life.

## Bring 'Em All Out

If you're planning on having the entire wedding party introduced before you, you can have a separate song, or several, for this, and there are different ways to bring 'em out:

- All the guys first, or all the girls first;
- Switching by gender (groomsman then bridesmaid, groomsman then bridesmaid, etc.);
- As one big group;
- As couples (like at the ceremony).

The most popular way for me to mark their entrance has been to play one song for the entire wedding party. I would either announce them as couples or one at a time, with the best man and maid/matron of honor going last, just as a sign of respect. I've also done a song for them to come out as one big group and then just announced them as "the wedding party." On rare occasions, I have snippets of songs, one for each person being introduced, though that can be hard for a DJ because they have to be quick in switching the song, especially if the next person getting introduced is rushing in quicker than they can be announced. They can be introduced with first and last names, with first names only, with nicknames or anything silly. Still another option is for the DJ to introduce the parents, flower girl(s) and ring bearer(s), siblings, and even your officiant if you so choose.

Whatever song you pick, though, make it fun and energetic, anything that will say *party time*. My suggestions include Bruno Mars's "Marry You," Black Eyed Peas' "I Gotta Feeling," Chris Brown's "Forever," Justin Timberlake's "Can't Stop the Feeling!" and Beyoncé's "Crazy in Love" featuring Jay-Z.

## Just the Two of Us

Photo by Oleg Parylyak/Dreamstime, ID 94460654

If you have a small wedding party or just really don't want to introduce everyone for whatever reason, then just have the DJ introduce you. There's no set rule that says everyone has to be introduced, and in my opinion it's more intimate that way.

Here's a tip: If there's only a short walk from the doors you're entering over to the dance floor, just make your grand entrance song your first dance song, especially if it has a good intro. If your walk is more than 20 feet, or if you just prefer to have two different songs for your entrance and your first dance, then have your DJ edit the song you're using to walk in. Get right to the meaningful parts of the song and avoid a long instrumental opening where the vocals are just coming in after you're already on the dance floor. Listen to the song you picked out, decide where you want it to start, then have your DJ edit it.

There are different ways to be introduced:

- Mr. and Mrs. Joe Smith;
- Joe and Lisa Smith;
- Mr. and Mrs. Joe and Lisa Smith;
- The Smiths.

Choose whatever you're most comfortable with. It doesn't necessarily have to be how you were introduced at the conclusion of the ceremony, but it can be. Some couples choose to mimic it; some choose to go a completely different route.

If you want to really make an impact for your grand entrance, use the DJ's mic from behind the scenes to introduce your own wedding party, then have the DJ introduce you. Imagine the guests trying to find the source of the voice before they realize it was you the whole time.

# 14

---

# The First Dance

Photo by IvashStudio/Shutterstock, ID 475919596

$\mathcal{I}$F A COUPLE WERE EVER TO TELL me "just play whatever" for their first dance, I would instead recommend that they take the time to find a song they both connect to. A DJ truly can't make this choice for them, because the song they pick will be the song that they will relate to for the rest of their lives. When an aging couple walks down the street in their twilight years and they hear that song playing softly in a small-town café, the man will whisper to his wife, "They're playing our song." *That's* the meaning of your first dance song, and no one else can pick it but you. The hard part is deciding on it, but once you do that you can:

- Shorten the song if you choose to;
- Have other couples join you halfway through;

- Have the DJ narrate your love story as you dance;
- Record special messages to each other to be played during your song;
- Even attend a dance class beforehand to really get your moves down.

Bubbly and energetic or simple and low-key, it's really about what you both are most comfortable with. I always tell my couples that, for this and any other formal dance, if they want to end any of them early, to just leave the floor and I will fade the song out from there. Maybe you even know a certain spot in the song that you want it faded at. Regardless, a good DJ will watch your dance as it's happening and will fade it out when the time is right. If they're busy scrolling their phone or looking through their files instead of watching the dance and it's only after you've already left the floor that the song starts to fade, it can be an awkward moment.

If you're a traditional person, then you probably feel like no other dancing should happen until your first dance is over. Or maybe you don't care when your dance occurs, but here's why you should care. Even if you have your timeline down on paper, it will differ radically once the day of the wedding actually comes around because there *will* be unforeseen delays. As a DJ, it is always my job to follow what the coordinator requests, since they're the ones getting paid to handle the timeline and all of the events associated with it. But as I've mentioned before, a DJ still has their favorite timelines. In my experience, the first dance is always best right after the grand entrance because at no other point at the reception will you have the full attention of your audience. Their eyes will follow you wherever you go at this point, so it just makes sense to have your first dance now and get it out of the way. Otherwise, it may not be as easy to pull you away later once you start mingling with your guests. I've done weddings where dinner was served right after the grand entrance, then the cake cutting and toasts were scheduled after the meal and the first dance didn't occur until later. It's not unheard of to do it this way, but I always find that it's just easier to get your dance out of the way as early in the night as possible. However, in saying that, I will reiterate that a DJ should *always* follow the coordinator's timeline, whatever that may be. A DJ should never be argumentative. That way, your first dance, and everything to follow, flows beautifully.

# 15

---

# The Dinner

Photo by DfrolovXIII/Shutterstock, ID 1059199631

$\mathcal{A}$T WHAT POINT IN THE NIGHT YOU have your dinner will largely depend on your caterer. For most weddings I've worked, dinner occurred either immediately following the grand entrance or right after the first dance. Your coordinator or the venue's on-site manager will know what's best for when and where to schedule it, but I would definitely recommend the dinner being done pretty quickly after your big entrance. You don't want to schedule all of the formal dances up front and wait until after all that to serve the food. Guests will be starving by that point, and besides, there won't be a lot to look forward to later in the evening to keep them around.

Regardless of what time dinner is set to begin, there are a few things your DJ should ask you about:

- Will there be a welcome message given?
- Is someone blessing the meal?
- Will the dinner be plated or buffet line?
- Are your tables being numbered?
- What is your preference for dinner music?

## Welcome Message/Blessing

A welcome message is an optional greeting that the couple, one of the dads, or the officiant can give, just to welcome the guests. It's not necessary, but is always a nice touch, especially if you combine it with the blessing. Most times the guests want to hear from you, but if either of you aren't fans of public speaking then someone else can speak on your behalf.

Generally speaking, if one of your dads is giving a welcome message, then he usually won't give a toast later on. But it's not strictly against the wedding etiquette if he does choose to do both.

Note: A welcome message isn't a toast; it's just a basic welcome and a thank-you.

The blessing can also be done by the person who's giving a welcome message, but it's not imperative that you have a blessing either. Most religious ceremonies, however, will include it.

Photo by Magryt/Dreamstime, ID 92479800

## Plated Vs. Buffet Line

As a DJ, I always love when the dinner is plated because it's very straightforward; I just start playing dinner music right away.

When a buffet line is set up, you'll have to decide how you want to release the tables and in what order. You always want to send the wedding party, immediate family, and all reserved tables through first. You should consider sending tables that have children or older guests next, just as a sign of respect.

It's very helpful to the DJ to have your tables numbered, especially if there's no coordinator going around and personally releasing guests to the buffet line. A word of caution, though: *Make sure* that the DJ announces, "Please wait until your table is released before heading to the buffet line." If table 5 decides to get in line before tables 3 and 4, you'll have an unnecessarily long wait at the buffet. It's best to invite no more than two or three tables through the buffet line at one time to avoid lines snaking between and around the tables. It can be very awkward if the line is weaving through a group of tables when those people are trying to eat and then you have other people standing there still waiting for their food. So just make sure your DJ is mindful of the "lunch line."

## Dinner Music

Pick out something nice and smooth, nothing too crazy and nothing too loud. Dinner is a time for guests to visit, talk, and enjoy their meal without any unnecessary chatter from the DJ. Your guests don't want to have to shout over the music in order to hold conversations, though of course they also will enjoy some nice music playing lightly in the background.

Here's some playlist suggestions.

For contemporary or Texas country classics: George Strait, Cody Johnson, Luke Combs, Pat Green, Flatland Cavalry.

For instrumentals: The Piano Guys, Brooklyn Duo, Vitamin String Quartet.

For coffee house/indie artists: Leon Bridges, Laufey, Norah Jones, Emily Hearn.

For classic crooners: Frank Sinatra, Dean Martin, Michael Bublé, Bobby Darin.

For Motown classics: The Temptations, The Four Tops, Marvin Gaye, Etta James.

## Make Dinner Service Lively

If you're wanting to add some creativity to the transition into dinnertime to make it more fun and to get your guests more involved, there are a variety of fun options you can include.

*TV theme trivia*: Have your DJ pick out snippets of popular TV themes; whichever table answers correctly first earns a trip to the buffet line.

*Bride and groom trivia*: Pick out some questions about the two of you, and let guests battle it out for the next table release through the line. However, don't let the wedding party chime in!

*Are you smarter than the wedding party?* This is where the wedding party *can* chime in. Members of the party can do battle against guest tables to see if they can outwit and outlast them to get their group to the food.

*Kissing couples*: Give the DJ a list of married couples in attendance, and throughout dinner service have everyone tap their drinking glasses for the next couple to kiss. Make sure you give your DJ the tables they'll be sitting at so that any given couple isn't at the buffet when the glasses clink. (Note: This only works with real glasses, not red Solo cups or beer cans!)

*Words of wisdom cards*: This is a great activity for your guests to do while they're waiting for dinner, or even during cocktail hour. Have them fill out their best advice and consider getting your DJ to read the funniest ones out loud.

*Shoe game*: This is best done toward the end of dinner when a bit of a lull can typically set in. It really gets the crowd's full attention because you never know what the answers will be. You and your groom will sit in two chairs, back to back, and exchange a shoe with each other. The DJ will ask questions and then you raise the shoe that you think corresponds with the question. Great laughs.

Photo by Andrei Zveaghintev/Dreamstime, ID 88103309

Remember, dinner doesn't have to be boring. It should be an enjoyable part of the night, with lots of hugs, mingling, light background music, and delicious food.

# 16

---

# The Cake

*B*EFORE I GET INTO A DISCUSSION OF the actual cake cutting, it goes without saying that, first, you have to find the cake. That means a lot of taste testing (but who's complaining?).

Jula Tragni, owner of Cakes by Jula, answered some cake-related questions for me. Even though a DJ is never involved in picking out a cake, I thought her comments would still be helpful here.

She's noticed that a lot of couples ask what the differences are between buttercream and fondant icing:

Fondant is a sugar dough, which is rolled out, then draped and molded over the cake. This is usually over a layer of buttercream. It is smooth and clean but does not taste as good as

107

buttercream and costs more. Brides like fondant for the look. Buttercream tastes better than fondant and costs less while it's not as smooth and clean as fondant.

I also asked her how far ahead in advance couples need to book their wedding cake. Jula says:

> Three to six months is a good guide. It is best if the following items are decided on before you set up a wedding consultation/ tasting with the bakery of your choice: venue; wedding colors/ theme; wedding dress; bridesmaid's dresses, flowers, and flower colors. You can consider options other than a "traditional" wedding cake like a cookie cake, dessert bar, macarons, and many other types of desserts.

Jula also suggests talking with your baker about the styles of cake you like. (But remember, this is your wedding; do what you want.) She says, "There are many options and you can pick a baker that will make your wedding cake what you are wanting, but if the baker will not do what you want, don't talk to them into doing something they aren't comfortable with. There's a good chance you will not be happy with the final product on your wedding day."

Now that you're a little more educated on actually picking out the cake, tasting it, and displaying it, now we jump forward to the cake on the wedding day.

Cutting the cake is traditionally the first task that you will complete together as a married couple, which is exciting in itself. So the music shouldn't be loud; in fact, it should primarily serve as background music. If it's thumping and bumping while you're cutting the cake, then it's way too loud. You need to be able to hear the venue manager, the coordinator, or the photographer telling you how you should be cutting the cake. Depending on when you're planning to cut the cake during the night, someone also needs to make sure that the cake knife is *on the table and ready*.

Photo by Wedding and Lifestyle/Shutterstock, ID #1166090509

There are two main ways you can do your cake cutting. The first is intimate style. This is done quietly without all the fanfare. The two of you simply go over to the cake table with just the photographer—no announcements, crowd, or specific song. You just stroll over there whenever you're ready to have it done.

Then there's the traditional way where the DJ announces, "OK folks, it's now time for Bob and Jane to cut the cake," or something to that effect. The guests will follow you to the cake table while the music is played at a pleasing level and the photographer gets in place. Just make sure that the DJ lets your guests know not to interfere with the professional photos, because after all, it's *those* photos that you're paying for, not the ones being taken on someone's phone.

My favorite place to schedule the cake cutting is not more than 30 or 45 minutes after dinner service, right before the toasts (if you're doing them). I like the cake to be cut before the toasts, because then while you're assembling guests and speakers for toasting, the venue can get to work on cutting up and distributing the rest of the cake for the guests. It will save you at least 30 minutes, which is a plus if the itinerary is running behind because the photographer wanted to slip outside with the two of you for sunset photos or if visiting with guests happened to go a little longer than you thought it would.

## The Cake Smash Sneak Attack

If you dare to try this, in order to pull it off, you have to have a best man and maid of honor that don't get upset too easily. So, the way this works is *after* the cake cutting but *before* passing slices out to the rest of the guests, you tell the two of them that you want to have a picture taken with them in front of the cake. You should probably have the two pieces of cake already in your hands, so that before the photographer snaps the pic, you push the cake in *their* faces. Make sure your photographer is ready for the capture!

## The Serenade

This one is a little bit more tame and doesn't involve making a mess on people that aren't expecting it. Simply speaking, you and your DJ come up with a song, and then he or she invites the guests, as they're watching you cut the cake, to sing along. (I would suggest a song like The Righteous Brothers' "You've Lost That Lovin' Feelin'.")

♪ ♪ ♪ ♪

You probably don't want to open up the dance floor immediately after you cut the cake. Give your guests a few minutes to have their dessert before they lace up their boogie shoes. Have your DJ play some fun tunes, maybe something "un-danceable" on your playlist. You might even want to slip into your dancing dress at this point, especially if the cake cutting got a little messy (even if you're telling yourself, "Oh, that's not happening").

But most of all, avoid putting the cake cutting too late in the itinerary. You may read wedding blog posts about how older guests will leave right after the cake cutting, so to keep them around, you should schedule the cake cutting after the dance floor has been opened. The thing is, if guests aren't being entertained, they will leave anyway, regardless of when and where you have the cake cutting scheduled. You want to get the most out of your timeline in accordance with the entertainment of your guests, and that's why I strongly suggest keeping the cake cutting around the dinner and the toasts. Don't read too much into other brides' social media posts; they may have not gotten the kind of cool DJ you've hired. Rely on your DJ instead.

# 17

## The Toasts

BEFORE THE TOASTING COMMENCES, THE DJ SHOULD remind guests to visit the bar for a refill or to grab a flute if there's champagne available. The main thing is that enough time, usually 10 to 15 minutes, is given for guests to get a fresh drink and for the photographer to get in place for the toasts. (Really, before *any* events at the reception take place, announcements need to be made so no one is caught off guard.)

You also have to think about who you want to have access to the microphone *before* the wedding. In theory, you might want to just open the floor to whoever wants to give a speech, but in my experience, that means you never know who might take the mic and what they might say. I did a wedding years ago where the grandfather of the groom took the mic and pretty much launched into a series of what I considered to be quite insulting remarks that were supposed to sound like playful banter. And as I was watching all this unfold, I was also watching the groom's face, which had no expression on it. But I could tell he was embarrassed.

There also may be coworkers or other family members who want to say a few words and will approach the DJ to ask for the mic, even if there's been no request for toast volunteers. It's up to you to approve or deny those requests, not the DJ. If you instructed the DJ to only allow members of the wedding party to speak, that's what they're supposed to honor.

If you want to play it safe, have the maid (or matron) of honor and best man speak, any other members of the wedding party, and either one or both of the fathers. Traditionally the father of the bride speaks last, but it really all depends on how you want it done and who you want speaking. When you've decided who's toasting, confirm the order that you want them to speak in, and then *make sure* they know when it's their turn to get the mic. Have them keep it short, nothing much longer than a couple of minutes. And please, discourage whoever is toasting from doing an actual mic drop. DJs hate that, and you don't want to be on the hook for having to replace their $500 mic because the best man wanted to make an impact.

When toasters have the mic, make sure they're holding it up to their lips when speaking. Too many times, people will hold the mic at their waist, so not only can the guests not hear them but it can also cause feedback if they're anywhere close to a speaker.

You should also remind them beforehand to raise their glass for the actual toast. At the end of some speeches, whoever's talking will often forget to say, "Raise a glass." It's not wedding law, but it's always the way a toaster should end their speech.

Videographers often suggest that the toasters use a mic stand with the mic firmly attached to it, because then it keeps the speaker in one place. Otherwise, it can be tricky to track a moving person with a camera. A stand also assures the speaker will be kept squarely in the great lighting that's been set up to ensure beautiful footage.

I would also advise you not to ask your DJ to cut off someone who's making a speech. I played a wedding once where the mother of the bride was on the mic giving her toast for maybe three or four minutes when the bride looked at me discreetly and gave me the cutoff sign. Let me be clear: I do *not* like cutting people off in the middle of talking, especially when it is a parent. So I hesitated, but again I got the cutoff sign from the bride. Finally I announced that we were moving on to the next toaster. The mother was furious, the crowd was also displeased, so I had to allow mom to continue, despite the bride's instructions. The dad gave me a stern talking-to in a not-so-nice way, and the bride never came forward to explain that it was her idea to cut off her mom.

So ultimately it falls on the speaker's shoulders to know how long to speak for. That's why I say to be mindful of who you're asking to toast you. Usually it's always safest to keep the toasts within the wedding party, because that way you'll know who's toasting and you can let remind them beforehand to keep it short and sweet.

## The Key Trick

I've done this little stunt numerous times over the years, and it's a great way to play a joke on the unsuspecting groom, if they're not the type to get angry too easily. However, this one only works if you've never lived together, if he's had his own house or apartment, and if you have other people willing to be in on the prank.

Before the wedding, you would put the plan in place for people you've chosen to pick up a blank key from the DJ at the wedding, usually during the cocktail hour. When it comes time for the toasts, usually the best man will announce that, since the groom is now off the market, anyone who still has an old key to his house/apartment/condo/etc. should bring it forward now. One by one, the people with the keys will come up and drop the keys on the table. Believe me when I say it can be hilarious.

♪ ♪ ♪ ♪

Technology has a great way of allowing absent family and friends to still have a part in your wedding even if they can't be there in person. I worked a wedding recently where the best man ended up not being able to attend the wedding because his sister's wedding happened to be scheduled on the same day, about two hours away. The original plan was for someone to read a note from the best man, but because I wanted to make it more special for the couple, I asked the bride to get the best man to send me a voice memo. I then edited it together with a little light piano music playing in the background. It came out perfect.

This is what it means for a DJ to go *above and beyond* to improve on something. Your DJ should be overflowing with ideas to make your wedding sizzle.

# 18

---

# Daddy/Daughter Dance

*A*FTER THE FIRST DANCE, THE SECOND MOST anticipated dance of the reception is your dance with dad. This moment always offers something meaningful, moving, and emotional because before your fiancé proposed to you, he asked your dad for your hand in marriage.

On your wedding day, your dad had the honor of walking you down the aisle.

On your wedding night, your dad gets to make a toast to his little girl and her new husband, as well as share a special dance with his baby under the ballroom lights, fighting back the tears. A beautiful moment shared between a father and his baby girl.

The whole day is something you've spent hours, even years, dreaming of, that fairytale wedding. Whatever you envisioned, it's now coming true. From a dad's perspective, this is the moment he's been excitedly awaiting yet partly dreading. It's bittersweet, but more on the sweet side. A very long time ago, the father/ daughter dance was done first, and it was the dad's way of "letting his little girl go" and "passing off" her hand to her new partner in her new life. It's rare nowadays for this dance to be scheduled before the first dance because so many wedding traditions have changed with the times.

When picking out the song you want to dance to with dad, it's important to consult with him. He'll either have valuable input on what to pick, or he'll put the job entirely on your shoulders. But it is still important to consult about that moment with him. It's not easy for dads to let go of their little girls. After all, he watched you grow from an infant to a toddler to a young woman, through soccer and softball practices to dance recitals to high school graduation and beyond. And now, today, he's giving you away. Nothing can replace these memories, of course, but picking out the song that you both will dance to at your wedding might help lessen the load.

Photo by Robert J. Gatto/Shutterstock, ID 300753533,
Photo by Lightfield Studios/Shutterstock, ID 1337330228

A dance like this only happens once in a lifetime, so make it special. Or, you can go the route that Lauren did prior to her 2020 wedding:

> I wanted to keep the songs with my parents a surprise. My stepdad came into my life when I was a teenager and has always been there for me when I needed him. It was no surprise that he would be having a dance with me. The version of "To Make You Feel My Love" by Garth Brooks had the perfect lyrics to show how much I appreciated all that he's done for me. Also a bonus, Garth was his favorite artist!

I've done a lot of weddings where a dad and a stepdad were both honored, sometimes to the same song, sometimes to a different one, but they always were cordial. There are always special circumstances with every wedding and every family, and you have to do what's best for your wedding, and that can also include finding a way to honor a deceased parent. You can either choose to honor his memory by having another close older man in your life to step in, or just forego it altogether.

The strong bond between father and daughter can create lasting memories, as was the case with Ali's wedding in 2013:

> As a little girl, most of us dream about our wedding day with our Prince Charming. You dream about the fancy decorations, the elaborate (delicious) cake, towers of food, beautiful lights, and fun music. All of your family and friends gathered around you to celebrate you becoming one with the love of your life. As you grow and mature, you begin to understand all of those take money, and lots of it. When the time to start planning your actual wedding arrives and you begin to create a budget, you quickly realize that you have to choose your priority must-haves and what you can live without.
>
> We decided that decorations weren't as important as the experience and fun of the night. And I'm so thankful that we

did. Planning out our flow of the night and special songs with our DJ took so much stress off of me on that night. It was time for the father/daughter dance, and I danced with my daddy for the first time in a very long time. We danced to "Butterfly Kisses" to let us reminisce about our life together when I was little. My dad was not a dancer, and definitely NOT an emotional person, but this special moment had us both in tears. He tried to spin me, which we didn't quite pull off, but we got a good laugh out of it. It was such a blissful, sweet moment shared between a daddy and his little girl. Little did I know, it would also be the last time we ever got to dance together.

Just eight months after our wedding, my dad unexpectedly passed away. I couldn't help but think that I was so unbelievably grateful that he got to walk me down the aisle, give me away, and share this wonderful dance with me before he became ill six months later. None of us knew that night what the year ahead would hold for us, but I will forever hold dear to all those beautiful memories; all of the most important people in our lives, together, all in honor of our union. It made me realize to not take any moment for granted; that the stress of the wedding going perfectly to plan really doesn't matter. Be in the moment. Soak up all the love . . . and have fun!

Handling the remembrances of the loss of one (or both) of your parents on one of the most special and memorable days of your life can be difficult. Here are a few song suggestions for honoring their memory:

♪ "I Loved Her First"—Heartland
♪ "My Little Girl" —Tim McGraw
♪ "Cinderella"—Steven Curtis Chapman
♪ "Give Me Away—Riley Roth
♪ "Dance with My Daughter"—Jason Blaine

# 19

---

# Mother/Daughter Dance

*A* GIRL ALWAYS NEEDS HER DADDY, BUT IT'S her mom that becomes her best friend through all of what life throws at her as she's growing into maturity. Breakups, homework, school dances, a first crush—mom deals with all of that throughout the years, but there isn't much offered to her on her daughter's wedding night.

That's where this dance comes in.

In the previous chapter, Lauren mentioned her special dance with her stepdad, but she also had this to say about her mom:

I not only wanted to show my appreciation for my stepdad, but a huge appreciation to the woman who has helped shape me into the person I am today, my mom. The song "My Little Girl" by Tim McGraw she always said she wanted to sing at my wedding when I was younger. I thought it would be the perfect surprise to ask her to dance following my father/daughter dance. She never expected it, and it was such a special moment at my wedding for us.

For this dance, whomever you choose to have this dance with, especially if it's a surprise, will bring tears to her eyes. There are so many great songs out there that you can use. My suggestions would include:

♪ "Mama's Song"—Carrie Underwood
♪ "The Perfect Fan"—Backstreet Boys
♪ "A Song for Mama"—Boyz II Men
♪ "The Best Day"—Taylor Swift
♪ "In My Daughter's Eyes"—Martina McBride

Whatever song you choose, and whoever is the recipient of this beautiful dance, it will be a joyous moment for the both of you. And here's a tip: Take the mic and say a few words to her before you start the dance. It'll make that sweet moment that much sweeter.

# 20

---

# Mother/Son Dance

Photo by DocPhotos/Shutterstock, ID 2427204629

FIRST STEPS. SKINNED KNEES. HOMEWORK AT THE kitchen table, late-night talks, hard lessons, quiet prayers.

From the moment he took his first wobbly steps, there was mom, always right there to cheer him on and pick him up whenever he fell, quietly teaching him how to stand tall. A mother's love truly shapes his first words, his first dreams, and the man he will eventually become, and no matter how old he gets, there's a part of him that will always need his mom—her encouragement, her wisdom, her steady hand.

The mother/son dance is a chance to honor that lifelong bond, to pause the whirlwind of the wedding day, and to share a few minutes of music, memories, and gratitude before he steps into this new chapter of his life.

Much like the daddy/daughter dance, this moment in time will be filled with love, happy tears, and so much emotion that there won't be a dry eye anywhere in the room. This dance also comes with the difficult task of picking out the right song. She may have a favorite; he may have something in mind. But whatever they decide, it will be perfect, because the song itself will say all that needs to be said.

Some suggestions:

♪ "My Wish"—Rascal Flatts
♪ "You'll Be in My Heart"—Phil Collins
♪ "Her Little Man"—Jami Grooms
♪ "Wildflowers"—Tom Petty
♪ "Landslide"—Fleetwood Mac

With any formal dance or parent dance, you don't have to be out on the dance floor for the entire length of the song. You can decide ahead of time when you'd like the DJ to fade it out, or whoever's dancing can just leave the floor when either one of you is ready for the dance to end. A glance at the DJ sometimes doesn't always work because, in my experience, it can be hard to tell if someone is intentionally glancing at me or just looking around the room, and I definitely never want to fade the song out early if someone isn't ready for the dance to end. So, the best way to cue a good fade is to hug and then leave the floor. That way, the DJ will know that they can begin the fade.

# 21

---

# New Parents Dance

Photo by Malysheva Liudmyla/Shutterstock, ID 750411637

*A*NOTHER OPTION THAT CAN BE ADDED TO the rest of the formal dances is the new parents dance. What better way to get acquainted with your new in-laws than to share a special dance with them at your wedding?

The dance starts with you dancing with your new father-in-law while the groom dances with your mom. This gives the "other" parents a chance to dance at your wedding and get a little of the spotlight. Even if you're already having a mother/daughter dance, you can still have this dance in order to include his dad. This one especially can be a short dance with a quick fade, basically just long enough to share some quality time, or of course you can dance to a complete song.

You can have as many or as few of the parent dances as you choose, but I would advise doing them all after dinner, cake, and toasts, right before the dance floor opens.

Some additional song suggestions for these in-law dances:

♪ "Isn't She Lovely"—Stevie Wonder
♪ "Lean on Me"—Bill Withers
♪ "Forever Young"—Rod Stewart
♪ "Count on Me"—Bruno Mars
♪ "You've Got a Friend"—James Taylor

This way, with a new parents dance, *all* the parents are included and no one feels left out.

# 22

---

# Other Family Dances

*W*EDDINGS AREN'T JUST ABOUT TWO PEOPLE JOINING their lives; they're also about families blending, bonds deepening, and relationships being celebrated.

Beyond the traditional parent dances, some couples choose this time of the reception to share a spotlight with other loved ones. Maybe the bride takes a moment to twirl with her brother who's been her lifelong protector, the groom shares a laugh-filled dance with his sister, or the parents spin across the floor with the children who made them a family long before the wedding day. These moments don't just honor the past; they also create memories that will be treasured long after the music fades.

## Siblings Dance

One brother, one sister, a whole group of siblings? There's no set rules when it comes to who you can dance with, especially if they're not directly involved in the wedding ceremony. Songs like this are sure to help make the moment memorable for everyone:

- ♪ "I'll Be There for You (Theme from *Friends*)"
  —The Rembrandts
- ♪ "Best Day of My Life"—American Authors
- ♪ "Sweet Disposition"—The Temper Trap
- ♪ "Halo"—Beyoncé
- ♪ "Something Just Like This"
  —The Chainsmokers and Coldplay

## Reverse Parents Dance

I call it the "reverse parents dance" because, essentially, the roles are reversed: You are now the parent dancing with your own child or children. Regardless of how old your children are now, it's especially lovely to share a special moment with them, even if just for a few minutes.

How incredibly emotional to be a bride dancing with your dad one moment and then to turn around as the parent dancing with your own children the next. It's not something not every bride gets to experience.

Suggestions for this sweet interlude:

- ♪ "Butterfly Kisses"—Bob Carlisle
- ♪ "Lullabye (Goodnight, My Angel)"—Billy Joel
- ♪ "You Are My Sunshine"—Johnny Cash
- ♪ "God Only Knows"—The Beach Boys
- ♪ "Sweet Pea"—Amos Lee

Photo by Stocknadia/Shutterstock, ID 23235424

# 23

---

# Anniversary Dance

*T*HE ANNIVERSARY DANCE IS ONE OF MY favorite ways to transition toward finally opening the dance floor to everyone, especially when you have a lot of couples in attendance. It's an almost guaranteed way to get the couples out on the floor while creating a sweet, memorable moment before the energy kicks in.

The best place to schedule the anniversary dance, if you choose to have it, is right after the parent dances. Emotions will already be running high after your dance with your dad and your hubby's dance with his mom, so the guests should be primed for a chance to dance with their significant other.

I've done the anniversary dance two different ways, and if you can't choose between them, it is possible to combine the approaches.

## The Removal

In this version, the DJ invites all of the married couples, including the newlyweds, onto the floor at the same time. One contemporary song will play first; all the couples have a chance to dance one through; and then a second song begins when the DJ will start asking couples to leave the floor. The DJ should gradually start calling out various categories of couples, for instance:

- "If you've been married longer than the newlyweds, keep dancing";
- "If you've been married five years or more, keep dancing";
- Then call out 10, 15, 20 years, and on up, until there's only one couple left dancing.

Once the song ends and that final couple finishes their dance, the DJ should then go out to the floor with the mic and let that couple give you their secrets for a long-lasting marriage. Make sure the photographer gets a photo with all four of you as well.

## The Reversal

Over the years, the reversal has become my personal favorite way to run the anniversary dance. It doesn't involve removing any couples from the dance floor (but then again it also doesn't culminate with a couple giving you their secrets). Here's how it works:

- The DJ invites couples married 50+ years to the floor first;
- The DJ invites those married for 40+, 30+, 20+, and 10+ years next;
- The bride and groom enter last to resounding applause.

You'll have a chance to watch as each couple is celebrated when it's their time join the crowd on the floor. Then when as you join as the last couple, you'll find yourselves surrounded by all of the couples who represent the journey ahead.

## Combine Both

For a more dynamic approach, or if you absolutely cannot decide between the two approaches, here's a way to combine them:

- The DJ starts the song with the bride and groom dancing alone;
- Then more couples are added in stages, beginning with those married fewer than 5 years, fewer than 10, fewer than 15, etc.
- The longest married couples will join last and can still give advice at the end.

If you go with this combined option, you now have a ton of options to play with. The DJ can then reverse the process and start removing couples by marriage length, or everyone can continue dancing together, filling the floor with love.

Here's another thing to consider: Some older couples may not be able to dance for too long, so that's another reason to go with the reversal. It keeps them on the floor just long enough to feel honored without tiring them out.

Whichever version of the anniversary dance you like best, anything can be changed about it, and you can make adjustments for however you want it to go. Then the only thing left is to pick out some music! My suggestions:

- ♪ "Tennessee Whiskey"—Chris Stapleton
- ♪ "Can't Help Falling in Love"—Elvis Presley
- ♪ "Can't Take My Eyes Off You"—Frankie Valli
- ♪ "L-O-V-E"—Nat King Cole
- ♪ "Stand by Me"—Ben E. King

Remember, when picking out the music for this dance, you'll want to choose a song so impactful that the older couples can't help but reflect on those days past when they first met, while the younger couples will look forward to the coming years together.

# 24

---

# Let's Dance!

*Y*OUR GUESTS SHOULD BE RARING TO GO by the time the dance floor opens, and probably even before that if your DJ did a good job getting everyone all warmed up with the anniversary dance. To really get things going, though, you'll need to pick out a song that will encourage and inspire everyone to come out to dance. "September" by Earth, Wind & Fire is my favorite go-to, but some other tunes that work well include:

- ♪ "I Gotta Feeling" or "Let's Get It Started" —Black Eyed Peas
- ♪ "Everybody (Backstreet's Back)"—Backstreet Boys
- ♪ "Celebration"—Kool & the Gang
- ♪ "Shut Up and Dance"—Walk the Moon

You could also officially kick off the open dancing by having your DJ call your entire wedding party out onto the floor. (A great song for this is "Mr. Brightside" by The Killers.) This will help really fill out the dance floor so that your photographer can get the best possible shots.

Every wedding is different, so guests may or may not start dancing right off the bat. But if the music is good and the DJ isn't talking all over it, they'll get out there. I generally don't start off with a line dance or a slow song. I find it's best to begin with something that signifies that the dance floor is open, and if you've got any big dancers in the crowd, it won't take long for other folks to follow them out there.

Photo by G-Stock Studio/Shutterstock, ID 1037566873

As the bride, you may take this moment when the first song begins playing to disappear for a minute to change into your dancing dress and boogie shoes. You definitely want to be comfortable when you're dancing, not worrying that someone is going to step all over the hem of your dress.

# 25

---

# Taking Requests

$\mathcal{B}$ECAUSE EVERY WEDDING CROWD IS UNIQUE, THE particular selection of songs that will get everyone on the dance floor will be unique as well. Allowing your DJ to take requests from guests can be a great way to keep the energy high and to help people feel included. However, this also requires a delicate balance; the DJ has to first and foremost honor *your requests* while still managing time and keeping the vibe flowing. This chapter will guide you through the pros and cons of taking requests and, ultimately, trusting your DJ to act with professionalism, kindness, and a bit of savvy so that your reception stays fun and memorable for everyone.

## Taking Requests: Pros

*Increased guest engagement:* Guests feel involved and excited when their favorite songs are played.

*Livelier dance floor:* Playing popular or personal requests can boost energy and get more people dancing.

*Personalized experience:* Requests can add variety and uniqueness that reflects the diverse tastes of the guests.

*Shows DJ flexibility:* A DJ who takes requests demonstrates adaptability and a guest-focused approach.

## Taking Requests: Cons

*Can disrupt the flow:* Requests can interrupt the carefully crafted timeline and vibe you've been working so hard to create.

*Inappropriate song risk:* Guests might ask for songs that don't fit the tone or have offensive content.

*Time management challenges:* Too many requests can slow down the set or cause your carefully paced playlist to get less attention.

*Conflicts with your preferences:* Guest requests might clash with the style of the other songs you want featured.

## Restricting Requests: Pros

*Maintains control over your playlist:* The DJ can ensure that the music will fit the style that you want.

*Keeps the flow smooth:* There's less chance of interruptions or awkward song choices that might stall the action on the dance floor.

*Avoids inappropriate or unwanted songs:* This goes a long way toward helping prevent songs with offensive lyrics, off-theme music, or awkward memories from sneaking into your special night.

*Better time management:* Your DJ can stick to the planned schedule without the potential for delays caused by too many requests.

*Respects your vision:* Taking no additional requests ensures that your wedding soundtrack will feel more personal and intentional.

## Restricting Requests: Cons

*Guests may feel excluded:* Some guests might feel less involved if they don't get a chance to hear their favorite songs.

*Missed opportunities for surprises:* Unique or unexpected songs can add fun and excitement when guests suggest them.

*Potential for disappointment:* Guests hoping to hear a specific song may be let down.

*Risk of a less dynamic playlist:* Without some of the variety that requests can bring, the music might feel predictable or repetitive.

♪ ♪ ♪ ♪

Now that you have more of a feel for the way that taking requests might affect your reception, you just have to weigh your options and decide what's more important. One final factor might help differentiate the two: If you feel you can trust your DJ's judgment. If you decide not to allow anyone to make requests, that may put your DJ in the position of having an unpleasant and unwanted confrontation with a guest. If your DJ is seasoned, they'll know how to handle requests and should be able to decide what songs are acceptable. Again, in your final consultation with your potential DJ, make sure these scenarios are discussed.

# 26

## Money Dance

$\mathcal{T}$HE MONEY DANCE, SOMETIMES CALLED "THE DOLLAR dance," depending on where you live, is a time-honored wedding tradition that brings the fun, the family, and the celebration. It gives your friends and family a chance to share a special moment with you, offering private well wishes and, yes, a few dollar bills while dancing together. The key is to have it early enough before a lot of guests start leaving.

It's also important to weigh the pros and cons before deciding if this dance is right for you. From my experience, money dances can either be a blast or a little bit awkward, so I recommend that you spend some time chatting with your DJ about it. Some guests might feel a little shy or uneasy about participating, and if it isn't well organized by your DJ, it could interrupt the flow of your reception. But with enough preparation and the help of a skilled DJ, it can become a smooth, enjoyable break that can re-energize the crowd during a slow moment on the dance floor. So if you know you have guests who love to dance and will eagerly join in, then go for it. Otherwise, think about whether it fits the vibe of your celebration and your comfort level.

Before the dancing starts, make sure to get some assistance with collecting funds; this is a good job for either the best man or the maid/matron of honor. They'll stand next to you to help regulate the lines as they come up. And don't forget to bring something to keep the money in! It can be something fun, such as a cowboy boot or hat, or something elegant, like a glass container. This small detail both adds charm and keeps the money safe and secure.

Depending on how long the guest lines are, your DJ will need a good three or four songs to play, maybe more. I wouldn't spend too long on the money dance, though, no more than 15 or 20 minutes so that you can move on to some more open dancing.

Song suggestions:

- ♪ "Why Don't We Just Dance"—Josh Turner
- ♪ "How Sweet It Is (To Be Loved by You)"
  —Marvin Gaye or James Taylor
- ♪ "With a Little Help from My Friends"
  —The Beatles or Joe Cocker
- ♪ "Love on Top"—Beyoncé
- ♪ "Piano Man"—Billy Joel

## A Nice Alternative

If you want the spirit of the money dance but prefer to skip the actual money exchange, consider simply inviting guests to share a dance with you, giving them the time to offer their words of wisdom (which they can even write down on cards handed out during cocktail hour). If nothing else, this can be a time for you to enjoy a quiet, meaningful dance together with some of your guests.

## Do's and Don'ts of a Successful Money Dance

DO discuss the money dance with your DJ well in advance.
DO pick enough familiar songs to allow everyone a chance to dance with you.
DO have the DJ recruit "money handlers" for the dance.
DO remind guests beforehand about the tradition so they know what to expect.
DO consider alternatives if the money exchange seems awkward.

DON'T force guests to participate; make it optional and fun.
DON'T choose too few songs in case the music runs out.
DON'T start the dance when the majority of guests are ready to leave or otherwise distracted.
DON'T let the money collection become chaotic; keep it organized and respectful.

With all this in mind, not to mention the right DJ and the right music, your money dance can be a big success!

# 27

---

# Line Dances

Photo by IvashStudio/Shutterstock, ID 461283832

$\mathcal{S}$OME BRIDES LOVE LINE DANCES; SOME HATE them; and some don't care about them either way as long as they fit into the overall wedding scheme. However, I will note that, if you tell your DJ that you don't want any line dances played at all, you may be restricting their ability to keep the floor full. And nine times out of ten, at least *one* guest will request either "Cupid Shuffle," "Wobble," and/or "Cha-Cha Slide."

From a DJ's perspective, a good line dance can really make the dance floor fill up. There are some songs that a DJ just *knows* will sizzle, and we use those as our back-pocket magic tricks. Speaking of "Cupid Shuffle," it's not just my most requested line dance, it's also my most requested song overall. There's a reason for that: People love it. It's an easy dance—the instructions are in the song!—and it's got a great beat. What I love is that it starts off with a bang, so it always makes for a great transition out of whatever song I have preceding it. I also like to wait to play it until the time is right: neither too early in the evening nor too late, when most people are starting to leave.

Line dances offer a chance for everyone to get on the floor, regardless of their dance skill level. They'll feel more involved and connected, and since most of these dances have simple, repetitive steps that guests can pick up quickly, that reduces a great amount of awkwardness as well. They're also great icebreakers, a way to refuel an empty dance floor. Some of the dances also have a nostalgic or cultural significance, adding even more fun to your celebration. Line dances can truly be a lifesaver for a DJ.

Aside from the aforementioned BIG THREE, here's some other popular options:

- ♪ "Bird Dance (Chicken Dance)"—The Emeralds
- ♪ "Copperhead Road"—Steve Earle
- ♪ "Boot Scootin' Boogie"—Brooks & Dunn
- ♪ "Macarena"—Los Del Rio
- ♪ "Boots on the Ground"—803Fresh
- ♪ "Footloose"—Kenny Loggins
- ♪ "Electric Boogie"—Marcia Griffiths
- ♪ "Cotton Eye Joe"—Rednex / "Cotton Eyed Joe" —Isaac Payton Sweat

As great as line dances can be, however, if overdone, they can seem monotonous and make the dance floor feel less spontaneous. For example, I might play "Cha-Cha Slide" or "Cupid Shuffle" early, then play some other, more danceable songs, and only a little later on during the rap/hip-hop portion of the music throw on "Wobble." A DJ should also never *force* a line dance on anyone. They should be spread out evenly and balanced.

# 28

## The Tosses

HE TOSSES: WILL YOU CHOOSE TO HAVE them? Some couples do, and some don't. Some may only have the bouquet toss. Depending on what you prefer, there are also a few alternatives to choose from.

### Bouquet Toss

The bouquet toss is the moment all of the young women at the wedding look forward to. There's the anticipation and excitement of going home with a souvenir, and possibly motivation for a future wedding. I always like doing the bouquet toss first, before the garter throw (if the couple is doing it), but the order really doesn't matter much should your DJ or coordinator decide to flip-flop them.

You don't want to do the tosses too early *or* too late. For best results, try to schedule them about 30 minutes to an hour before the end of the reception. But, you may need to move them earlier in the night if guests, especially the girls, start to leave. For a good bouquet toss that look great in photos, you need *at least* seven or eight girls and young women. I've worked plenty of weddings where, after watching the room, I realized needed to get the tosses started earlier than originally scheduled. Your DJ should be able to make that call as well, but if neither the DJ nor your coordinator is paying attention, then you may need to decide for them.

Also, be mindful about any kind of physical obstructions that might be the recipient of your toss rather than a happy girl. I assure you, a misfire will *not* look good in photos. For example, I've frequently worked one wedding venue where the ceilings aren't any more than eight feet high. It's a nice place otherwise, with an outdoor deck area where the ceremonies can be held;

however, with those low ceilings, I would always have to suggest that the bride (and the guests) go *back* outside to do the bouquet toss out on the deck. Trying to do the toss inside there is nearly impossible; you just can't do a proper toss unless you wing it sidearm. If you hit the ceiling, the bouquet starts to disintegrate. And if there are any low-lying chandeliers in your space, they are not your friend either, for obvious reasons. So you want to make sure you have enough room when tossing so that your bouquet will clear any hopefully minor obstructions. I've seen too many disasters happen too many times. So when you take your final walkthrough at your venue, be sure to scope out the location where you might have the bouquet toss to make sure there won't be any major problems on the big day.

If by chance there aren't enough single, unmarried women at the wedding, you can always ask *all* the women, regardless of marital status, to participate in the toss rather than not doing it at all.

Song suggestions:

- ♪ "Girls Just Want to Have Fun"—Cyndi Lauper
- ♪ "Single Ladies (Put a Ring on It)"—Beyoncé
- ♪ "Man! I Feel Like a Woman!"—Shania Twain
- ♪ "Gimme! Gimme! Gimme! (A Man After Midnight)" —ABBA
- ♪ "Where Them Girls At"—David Guetta, feat. Nicki Minaj & Flo Rida

## Don't Stop the Dancing

If dance floor is already packed but you need to do the bouquet toss, why break things up? Bring the bouquet out and have your DJ make the announcement before switching right over to whatever song you picked out for the toss. You'll already have the ladies out there dancing, and tossing the bouquet while they're out there will make them lose their minds.

## The Presentation

Photo by Kyryk Ivan/Shutterstock, ID 1609422910

Maybe you don't necessarily want to toss the bouquet, but you still want to present it to someone, either publicly or privately. For example, you can give it to your mom at the end of your mother/daughter dance, if you're doing one. Or maybe there's someone else you have in mind for it. Maybe your wedding day falls on your best friend's birthday and you want to give it to her, or you want to present it to your maid of honor because she's gone above and beyond to make your wedding day perfect. Or, you could take a quiet moment to present it to your grandmother. *Don't let yourself be talked into a bouquet toss if you'd prefer to just present it to someone.*

## Garter Toss

Some couples opt to omit the garter toss from their itinerary, because unlike the bouquet toss which can be very sweet, the removal part of it can get a little risqué. But of course many couples still do include it. I've even seen grooms choose to forego the removal altogether and just throw the garter.

Photo by Bogdan Sonjachnyi/Shutterstock, ID 582985753

If you *are* having the full-blown garter toss that includes the removal, someone will need to make sure there's a chair on the center of the dance floor following the bouquet toss. This can usually be done by the maid of honor, the photographer, or the coordinator.

You might think that your fiancé is *much too shy* to remove the garter, but you may be in for a surprise. During this event many grooms just seem to be in the moment like an actor on Broadway. He might even do a little dance on his own before getting down to business.

As for picking out music, you can either pick one song for both the removal and the toss or you can select separate songs for each. One song is usually fine, since it doesn't take but 30 seconds to pull off the garter, but again, I've seen it done both ways.

There are some really good songs that fit perfectly for the garter removal but not so much for the toss:

♪ "Let's Get It On"—Marvin Gaye
♪ "Thong Song"—Sisqó
♪ "Legs"—ZZ Top

♪ "The Stripper"—David Rose
♪ "Cherry Pie"—Warrant

Then for the toss, there's some music that's uniquely well suited for that moment:

♪ "Bad Boys (Theme from *Cops*)"—Inner Circle
♪ "It's Raining Men"—The Weather Girls
♪ "Save a Horse (Ride a Cowboy)"—Big & Rich
♪ "Whatta Man"—Salt-N-Pepa with En Vogue
♪ "Sharp Dressed Man"—ZZ Top

The DJ won't need a full song for either the removal or the toss, just about 30 to 45 seconds. But again, it's completely up to you if you decide to pick two songs or just one for both.

If you just want to have one song for both, try one of these:

♪ "SexyBack"—Justin Timberlake
♪ "Theme from *Superman*"—John Williams and the London Symphony Orchestra
♪ "Theme from *Mission: Impossible*"—Lalo Schifrin
♪ "One Way or Another"—Blondie
♪ "Hot Hot Hot"—Buster Poindexter

Unlike the gals, the guys might not be quite as giddy to get out there and catch the garter. Nine times out of ten, the guys want to look cool, which means they'll be standing around with a beer in one hand and the other neatly tucked into his pocket. Then they'll *reluctantly* grab for the garter if they want to be the winning catcher.

Just make sure your photographer takes a photo of all four of you together: the bride, the bouquet catcher, the groom, and the garter catcher. It shouldn't just be you with your bouquet catcher then the groom with the garter catcher, separately.

## The Switch-Up

If you want to spice up the tosses and really play up the hilarity for your guests, try the switch-up. Here's how it works.

Plan to do the garter toss first. Right before you sit in the chair, you switch places with your groom. Then you raise *his* pant leg and remove the garter that he's wearing. From there, you can throw the garter to the guys before your groom throws the bouquet to the girls. Or, you can throw the garter to the girls and he'll throw the bouquet to the guys.

If you do the switch-up, try to keep it a secret between just you and him. I promise, your guests will be talking about it for years.

## The Football Toss

A great upgrade to the basic garter toss is to get a mini football with his favorite team's logo on it, then wrap the garter around the football before tossing it to the guys. They'll be sure to catch it then! To make it even more special, sign the ball as a couple. It will be a wonderful souvenir for whoever catches it.

## Make Him Dance

For another pre-garter removal option, don't make it easy on him! Make him earn the garter by doing a sultry, sexy dance of his own before you allow him to continue with the garter removal. Get the crowd into it and ask them to applaud when they feel that his dancing is good enough to continue.

## The Handcuffs

Ask someone like the best man or a policeman friend to come in and handcuff the groom. Then it really becomes a challenge to get that garter, but what great photos you can get. Make it even *more challenging* than it already will be by making him dance for you first while handcuffed.

Since the tosses are typically the final spotlight events before your last dance, just be sure to schedule them for a time later in the night when most of the guests are still present so you can end the night on a high note.

But remember: You get to decide whether you want to do both tosses, just the bouquet, a special presentation, or nothing at all. It's your wedding, your call. These moments are meant to be fun, not forced.

# 29

## The Last Dance

Photo by Maxbelchenko/Shutterstock, ID 597369794

*I* ASKED JENNIFER, A BRIDE I WORKED WITH in 2014, what *one thing* remains the most memorable for her every time she looks back on her wedding.

The most memorable moment for me was the last dance. Many of our family members and friends had left because it was a Sunday night and getting quite late. We still had the venue for an additional hour, but seeing as how the attendees had rapidly thinned out, we decided to speed things up. I remember feeling this strange mix of happy and sad; happy because as I swung around with my husband in my arms, I could see my closest friends cheering us on. Then there was sad because this moment that took a year of planning, and even longer for saving, had finally ended. I knew that dance marked the end of a once-in-a-lifetime event for me. And I remember tearing a bit during the last few turns because I wished the music, the lights, the presence of so many people I loved . . . just that entire moment could last forever.

*The last dance.* I always call it "the last dance of the evening but the first dance of the rest of your lives." Because when you think about it, it is. It's the song that sends you out into your next chapter together.

The point of the last dance is for everyone to join you for one last big get-together. If the photographer is still around, it also makes for one or two more great photo ops.

It always helps for the DJ to at least mention that the last dance is about to occur. Sometimes the most person who needs to hear this announcement most is you! Maybe you're in the ladies' room changing into your after-party dress. But also, maybe the maid of honor is loading decorations into your car or there's a group of guests outside chatting. My point here is that you need to ensure your DJ will make that announcement.

The song you choose for your last dance should leave your guests with a memorable tune in their heads that they'll be humming or singing on the way home. My suggestions:

- ♪ "Closing Time"—Semisonic
- ♪ "One More Time"—Daft Punk
- ♪ "Piano Man"—Billy Joel
- ♪ "(I've Had) The Time of My Life"—Bill Medley and Jennifer Warnes
- ♪ "Don't Stop Believin'"—Journey
- ♪ "Good Riddance (Time of Your Life)"—Green Day
- ♪ "Save the Last Dance for Me" —Michael Bublé
- ♪ "Don't Stop Me Now"—Queen

Another fun option is to repeat your first dance song as your last dance song and let your couples dance to the song they watched you dance to earlier. It gives you a chance to dance again to the same song, but only this time they get to dance alongside you.

## Circle of Love

When it's done right, a circle of love looks amazing. It starts with the bride and groom in the middle of the dance floor, dancing to whatever song they've picked out, and then the remaining guests surround the newlyweds in a *circle of love*. Maybe they'll circle around, then go in closer and back out again, whatever they're feeling in the moment. And sometimes after a verse or two, couples will break off and dance right along with you.

You can even do what's known as the enhanced circle of love. It's organized much the same way, but only this time, the guests will pass around the mic and share their best and sweetest sentiments with you as you dance. It's almost like one big circular toast with music, and the words that people speak are timeless.

# 30

---

# Wrapping Up
# the Reception

$\mathcal{W}$HEN THE LAST DANCE HAS ENDED, BUT before it's time for your guests to head out to wherever you're having your big send-off, there may be some announcements for your DJ to relay to your everyone.

## Last Call

Find out from your bartender what time they're planning to close up and have your DJ make the announcement for last call. This notification is typically given about 20 to 30 minutes before the last dance to give people enough time to get one more drink. The main thing is, you don't want your guests going over to the bar when they're supposed to be lining up outside for the send-off.

## Midnight Snack

Sometimes couples will serve a special little snack toward the end of the reception. It could be something simple like chips and dip or churros. Or you could bring in a taco truck. At one of the weddings I worked a few years ago, the couple even brought in a bunch of Whataburgers. Not everyone does a midnight snack, but it can be a nice gesture. After a long night of drinking and dancing, guests will need some fuel to round out the night, especially since dinner was probably at least three hours before.

## The After-Party Plan

Photo by Neirfy/Dreamstime, ID 321712975

The party also doesn't have to end here! Maybe you'll move on to the pub down the street or the hotel bar, but whatever you have planned, make sure the DJ is in the loop. They shouldn't wait until the last song of the night to let everyone know that there even *is* an after-party.

Recently I did a wedding where the couple were having an after-party down the street, but they didn't want people to drive due to excessive drinking and other safety issues. So they arranged for charter buses to leave the hotel every 10 to 15 minutes to take guests to and from the other location up until midnight. But in order for people to take advantage of that service, they needed to plan ahead for it. So it's OK for the DJ to repeat an important announcement about something like that, sometimes even two or three times. I've noticed that people don't really pay attention to what the DJ is saying unless the music stops; at that point you have their full and undivided attention.

I was at a wedding where the couple had covered the costs of Uber rides for guests leaving the reception, and it was such a wonderful gesture. I asked Angela and Clint, the couple, where they thought of that idea.

"Clint had been to some events in the past that offered Uber services to guests," Angela said. "Since we were serving alcohol with an open bar, we strongly felt it was a responsible service to our guests to make sure everyone made it home safely."

# 31

---

# The Private Dance

*T*HE PRIVATE DANCE HAS BECOME QUITE POPULAR over the last few years, something a lot of couples are choosing to do. Since it only involves the couple, and the music is at a lower volume, it gives the photographer a chance to take some more great shots of the two of you dancing.

For just this moment, you can slow things down and take it all in. There are no eyes watching you, no applause, just a quiet moment that's privately shared. Look around and appreciate all the excitement, all the dancing, and all the laughter, joy, and happy tears. Take a moment together to look back on a beautiful wedding that was infused with energy and love. A great song for this private dance would be "Joy of My Life" by Chris Stapleton.

Then when the song is over, quietly kiss and get ready to run through the doors for your big send-off, where the guests are waiting to scream out your names and applaud one last time.

# 32

---

# The Big Send-Off

*Y*OUR GRAND FINALE.

The guests are lined up outside in two single-file lines awaiting your exit. The photographer is at the end of the line with the camera pointed at the door. Everyone is ready.

This is the last impression you'll have of your wedding day: a beautiful experience that now draws to a close. Whether you've envisioned a romantic sparkler tunnel, a colorful ribbon wave, bubbles floating through the night air, or something completely unique, this moment is about celebration, excitement, and sending you off into married life *in style.*

When planning your send-off, try to keep in mind the energy of the night and the size of your guest list. You might not want to wait until the very end of the reception as you risk some guests leaving early. So your photographer may opt to go with a faux send-off earlier in the evening while the majority of your guests are still there.

Work with your photographer, DJ, and coordinator to ensure *everyone* knows where to be and when, and remember to consider safety for any hazardous items like sparklers, confetti, or glow sticks (which all require a bit of coordination). Be sure to also check with your venue to see what's allowed on the property before buying anything for specific the send-off.

The finishing touch is a great exit song for your walk out the door. Use the same song you used for your grand entrance, or put an exclamation point on a day that you will never forget with something like "Cowboy Take Me Away" by The Chicks or "Can't Stop the Feeling!" by Justin Timberlake.

# 33

---

# After the Wedding

*T*HE WEDDING IS OVER, THE GUEST BOOK is packed away in a box, and the dance floor is empty, with nothing but memories and emotions remaining. But your relationship with your vendors doesn't have to end just yet. In fact, your DJ *should* reach out to you sometime after the wedding to make sure everything was to your satisfaction. A follow-up can go a long way; it shows that you weren't just another job but someone that they cared enough about to make sure you were happy with their services.

Leaving a review is one of the most valuable gifts you can give your vendors, including your DJ, after the wedding, but don't feel like you need to do it right away. You both will need time to recuperate from the last several months of meetings, cakes tastings, playlist creation, picking out photo packages, and deciding on how many RSVPs to send out. You're still on that wedding high, though you will certainly want a quiet place to rest and relax a bit, whether it be at home or on an island somewhere in the tropics.

## Why Reviews Matter

Every review matters. Your review can help other couples make informed decisions. Your review helps vendors grow their business in order to continue doing what they love. So please post a review on whichever platform you first connected on, whether it was Google, Zola, The Knot, or social media. Each review helps get your DJ and other vendors closer to the next level of their business, including yearly awards and other recognition. Your review is also proof that their hard work and dedication to your wedding made a real difference. Be sure to mention specific details if you can; that will make the biggest impact on folks reading them later.

## Not a Five-Star Experience

So maybe your experience with your DJ wasn't perfect. They played the wrong song for your first dance, didn't play any of the songs you requested, played explicit music without your approval, or they talked a ridiculous amount of time on the mic instead of letting the music play. Maybe your DJ was just horrible and you don't want to subject other couples to the kind of disaster that you had to experience.

First, consider reaching out to them directly before posting a review lower than 5 stars. Most wedding professionals will want the chance to fix any issues or clarify misunderstandings so that they can improve on their work. If they have consistently received 5-star reviews, a lower rating will bring down their average, so reach out to them first before you comment publicly. If they don't care to resolve your displeasure, then it's up to you to protect other couples from a bad experience.

## Share Some Photos with Your DJ

If your photographer shared some truly incredible photos with you, think about sharing some of those dancing shots with your DJ. It's not always easy for a DJ to take pics of their own while they're actively spinning music, so any photos that you can either tag them in or share with them for their own social media pages or website will be an amazing way to thank them further.

## Closing Thoughts

While your wedding day may have been the grand finale, the relationships that you built over the last several months will continue to contribute to your *happily ever after.* You have the chance now to not only help the people who helped you but to also be a part of making *someone else's* wedding day as magical as yours.

Photo by Nopparat Nambunyen/Shutterstock, ID 618709718

# ABOUT THE AUTHOR

*D*AVID CAMPO HAS SPENT OVER 25 YEARS immersed in the world of weddings, helping couples create unforgettable celebrations. With decades of experience coordinating music, timelines, and events, he has seen firsthand what makes a wedding flow smoothly—and what can go hilariously sideways. His insights come from real-life experience, giving couples practical advice they can trust.

A passionate advocate for helping brides and grooms take control of their wedding day, David now offers Virtual DJ Coaching for couples looking for guidance. Through his writing and coaching, he shares tips on planning, timelines, and working effectively with vendors to ensure the day runs seamlessly.

When he's not helping couples plan their perfect celebration, David enjoys spending time with family, reading, writing, listening to music, and recreational drumming.

You can find him online at spinmajic.com.

# YOUR WEDDING DJ, ANYWHERE

If you absolutely loved the ideas in this book and now are convinced you really need a pro in your corner, author David Campo offers **Virtual DJ Coaching**. During these quick one-on-one sessions, he will guide brides on:

♪ Picking and vetting the right local DJ

♪ Building a smooth, stress-free timeline

♪ Curating music for every key moment

♪ Communicating effectively with your DJ so nothing gets missed

♪ Which special songs he can make edits to, just in case your DJ can't

♪ Assembling playlists with ease

♪ And more!

With his coaching to assist you, you'll have no trouble getting the most out of your local DJ, no matter who they are, and avoiding a bad experience.

Plus, he will remain available to answer any and all questions up until your wedding day. Think of it as having a wedding DJ wingman in your back pocket.

Reach out at www.spinmajic.com.

*"I've got your back, even if I'm not on the dance floor."*

Photo by Nopparat Nambumyen/ Shutterstock, ID 1326343706